Understanding Mexico's Security Conundrum

Unlike other analyses which aim to explain the notion of national security in Mexico and at the same time address the security challenges facing the country, this short text describes the distinction between national, internal and public security in Mexico. It is the first book to provide detailed analysis on Mexico's security policy and its long-term consequences.

Mexican scholar and practitioner Augustin Maciel-Padilla contends that the absence of a clear understanding of the complexities and sophistication of the concept of national security has the potential to aggravate security conditions in Mexico. Achieving a proper understanding allows for a better guidance in confronting the grave insecurity facing the country, and for addressing other issues such as human rights, democracy and the country's international exposure. Maciel-Padilla reasons that Mexico is required to formulate a comprehensive, long-term, security strategy, and with this book he proposes a contribution towards that long-term goal.

Understanding Mexico's Security Conundrum will be essential for scholars, students and policy makers.

Agustin Maciel-Padilla is Head of the Border Affairs and Security Section at the Mexican Embassy in Belize. In the Government of Mexico, Dr. Maciel-Padilla has served in the Consulate General in El Paso, Texas, as officer in charge of border security affairs. His assignments have also included security advisor to the Undersecretary for North America at the Ministry of Foreign Affairs, and assistant to the Political Affairs Section at the Mexican Embassy to the United Kingdom.

Routledge Advances in International Relations and Global Politics

Mexico's Drug War and Criminal Networks
The Dark Side of Social Media
Nilda M. Garcia

Transnational Labour Migration, Livelihoods and Agrarian Change in Nepal
The Remittance Village
Ramesh Sunam

A Middle East Free of Weapons of Mass Destruction
A New Approach to Nonproliferation
Seyed Hossein Mousavian and Emad Kiyaei

Weak States as Spheres of Great Power Competition
Hanna Samir Kassab

Understanding Mexico's Security Conundrum
Agustin Maciel-Padilla

Exploring Base Politics
How Host Countries Shape the Network of U.S. Overseas Bases
Edited by Shinji Kawana and Minori Takahashi

United Nations Financial Sanctions
Edited by Sachiko Yoshimura

For information about the series: https://www.routledge.com/Routledge-Advances-in-International-Relations-and-Global-Politics/book-series/IRGP

Understanding Mexico's Security Conundrum

Agustin Maciel-Padilla

NEW YORK AND LONDON

First published 2021
by Routledge
52 Vanderbilt Avenue, New York, NY 10017

and by Routledge
2 Park Square, Milton Park, Abingdon, Oxon, OX14 4RN

Routledge is an imprint of the Taylor & Francis Group, an informa business

Library of Congress Cataloging-in-Publication Data
A catalog record for this title has been requested

ISBN: 978-0-367-42412-1 (hbk)
ISBN: 978-0-367-82400-6 (ebk)

Typeset in Times New Roman
by codeMantra

I dedicate this book to the memory of Professor Jose Thiago-Cintra who always encouraged and supported my pursuit of Security Studies.

Contents

Acknowledgments

I would like to recognize the generosity of Rodrigo Bustamante, Marcos Pablo Moloeznik, Erubiel Tirado, Saul Sandoval and Reynaldo Ortega, for criticizing the initial project as well as the manuscript of this book and for asking relevant questions. Thank you all for your time, for your pertinent comments and observations.

I express my deep and sincere gratitude to Juan Alberro who, during our long and inspiring conversations in Madrid in 2019, encouraged me to complete this enterprise. Special mention deserves Marco Mena for his friendship and for his invaluable support that allowed me to participate in a series of academic events in order to discuss sections of my research. My heartfelt appreciation for his never-ending kindness.

My warmest thanks to el Colegio de la Defensa Nacional and the Centro de Estudios Superiores Navales in Mexico City for the opportunity to visit in February 2020, and for their renowned hospitality and enlightening discussions. I also thank the latter for granting me online access to the Biblioteca Naval to collect sources of information for this project. Contact with Secretaria de Marina/Armada de Mexico was facilitated by Captain Alberto Perea Marrufo, Naval Attache to the Mexican Embassy in Belize. I appreciate very much his assistance. I also thank the George C. Marshall European Center for Security Studies for allowing me to use its Online Library as Alumni.

I am very thankful to Natalja Mortensen for her faith in me and to Charlie Baker for guiding me through the complex publication process, both at Taylor and Francis Group. Thank you for your trust. Finally, my profound gratitude for the support and love of my family, my parents, Agustin and Elizabeth, my wife Margarita, and my daughters, Astrid and Mirel to whom I promised I will make up for missed opportunities to have fun while I was working on this book.

Abbreviations

ALADI	Latin American Integration Association
ANR	National Risk Agenda
AMLO	Andres Manuel Lopez-Obrador
APEC	Asia-Pacific Cooperation Mechanism
APPRIs	Agreements for the Promotion and Reciprocal Protection of Investments
ATF	Bureau of Arms, Tobacco and Firearms
AWB	Federal Assault Weapons Ban
CIA	Central Intelligence Agency
CESNAV	Center for Higher Naval Studies
CISEN	Center for Investigation and National Security
CNI	National Intelligence Center
COVID-19	Coronavirus SARS CoV-02
CSN	National Security Council
CSS	Critical Security Studies
CODENAL	National Defense College
DEA	Drug Enforcement Administration
DFS	Federal Directorate of Security
DISEN	Directorate of Investigation and National Security
DTOs	Drug Trafficking Organizations
ESISEN	School for Intelligence and National Security
FBI	Federal Bureau of Investigation
FTAs	Free Trade Agreements
GAFES/GANFES	Army Air/Amphibious Special Forces Unit
GDP	Gross Domestic Product
HLCG	High-Level Contact Group
HVTs	High-Value Targets
IMRED	Matias Romero Institute for Diplomatic Studies
IR	International Relations

ISIS	Import Substitution Industrialization Strategy
JTF-4	Joint Task Force No. 4
LEAs	Law Enforcement Agencies
LSN	National Security Law
MORENA	National Regeneration Movement
NAFTA	North America Free Trade Agreement
NORTHCOM	United States Northern Command
OAS	Organization of American States
OECD	Organization for Economic Cooperation and Development
OIP	Political Information Office
PAN	National Action Party
PGR	General Attorney's Office
Plan DN	National Defense Plans
PND	National Development Plan
PRI	Institutional Revolutionary Party
SEDENA	Secretary of National Defense
SEGOB	Secretary of Goverment/Ministry of the Interior
SEMAR	Secretary of the Navy
SSPC	Secretary of Security and Citizen Protection
UMSCA	Agreement between the United States of America, the United Mexican States and Canada
UN	United Nations
WTO	World Trade Organization

Introduction

This book is the outcome of study and reflection on Mexico's national security. This process made it possible to identify a lack of a strategic perspective on the subject and, thus, to underline the importance of planning for the long-term.

There is no strategic outlook due to the fact that debates on "national security" in Mexico miss the point that the concept has first, and foremost, an international dimension, as its origin can be traced back to "political realism", one of the most influential International Relations (IR) theories. Public discussion on the subject usually reveals confusion regarding the distinction among "national", "internal", and "public" security, while it is also common to find the term indistinctively associated with the armed forces, intelligence, and political espionage, or interpreted as the security of the regime.

Both the legal framework that treats internal security as part of national security and the fact that drug trafficking transformed itself from a health issue into a public security matter, and into a national security threat, are two complications that have also contributed to the confusion. Analyses on national security in Mexico, however valuable as they are, tend to focus on separate aspects of the issue such as the notion, structures, processes, and threats, without systematizing all this information to provide the country with a comprehensive view centered on the external environment. This challenge was identified more than a decade ago (Maciel 2002), and this book intends to further contribute to addressing this problem.

Mexico's most relevant national security concern in the last decades has been the significant number of victims that has resulted from drug-related violence. In strict terms, drug trafficking is a national security issue because of its obvious transnational character, but also because it affects each of the components of the Mexican state (i.e. people, institutions, and territory).

Even though drug trafficking can be understood as just one aspect of an integrated global drug market (the other being demand/consumption), Mexico has for long adopted the US emphasis on the supply side of the equation by dealing with it within its own territory. This has occurred at a high cost in terms of lives, and exposing its armed forces – a key institution to the country's political stability – to corruption and violation of human rights accusations, without effectively containing the challenge. Drug trafficking in Mexico, therefore, has affected not only its social fabric, but also the integrity of a fundamental institution of the state.

After 71 years of Institutional Revolutionary Party-rule (PRI), political alternation in 2000 (Vicente Fox from the right-wing National Action Party [PAN] was elected President) led to political fragmentation, and in this context state and local governments found it difficult to abide by centrally designed security policies (Cerda-Ardura 2011). Later on, the strategy of striking at high-value targets (HVT) under President Felipe Calderon – also from the PAN – contributed to the division of these organizations (Felbab-Brown 2013). It led to an increase in the already present competition among them for territory and the lucrative corridors to the north, fostering inter- and intra-cartel conflict, and confrontation between these organizations and the security forces.

The PRI's return to power with President Enrique Peña-Nieto in 2012 did not make a difference in addressing the challenge. Changes in the security sector – the Secretary of Public Security was merged into the Secretary of Government/Ministry of the Interior (SEGOB), and the consolidation of a law enforcement and criminal investigations data base was abandoned (Plataforma Mexico 2018) – only worsened the situation. The administration ended up with a significant level of homicides, as it recorded a total of 156,437 cases, 34,824 more than in the Calderon presidency (Migueles 2019).

On December 1, 2018, a new political alternative came to power taking advantage of widespread social discontent generated by years of violence and corruption. Determined to carry out Mexico's "Fourth Transformation", which required dealing with insecurity, it created high expectations. By its tenth month in office, nevertheless, homicides under the new administration numbered 28,741, in a trend that contributed to portray 2019 as "the most violent year in the recent history of Mexico" (Redaccion 2019a).

Since the presidential campaign, Andres Manuel Lopez-Obrador (AMLO), the leader of the National Regeneration Movement (MORENA), began to publicly discuss "out of the box" approaches to deal with violence by correctly assuming that what Mexico required was an integral security policy to deal with insecurity. His approach, nevertheless, faced significant challenges. AMLO presented controversial proposals such as legalizing marijuana in the country and opium poppy production for the legal market, as well as pardon for low-level members of criminal organizations through the submission of an Amnesty Law to Congress, a plan whose implementation seemed problematic in terms of moral, legal, rule-of-law, and rights of victims dilemmas (Felbab-Brown 2019: 3a). This initiative, however, was approved for discussion on the floor by the Chamber of Deputies on December 2019 (Redaccion 2019b).

The most pressing challenge, nevertheless, is the fact that AMLO's government shows the same conceptual misunderstanding as its predecessors regarding national security mentioned earlier, which, in turn, represents a key obstacle to the formulation of a broader and comprehensive strategy to confront insecurity. This confusion was evident in the fact that the discussion of security matters on behalf of the new administration was led by the then-designated head of the reinstated Secretary of Security and Citizen Protection (SSPC) who, far from circumscribing himself to law enforcement matters, dealt with issues affecting the armed forces. He also supervised the initial proposal to disband Mexico's national intelligence agency (Center for Investigation and National Security-CISEN), because of allegations of political espionage (Redaccion 2018), to create instead a new organization under his own Secretary (that would naturally emphasize crime prevention and investigation activities), wasting the opportunity, therefore, to fulfill the urgent need for Mexico to have a foreign intelligence service, given the country's increasing international vulnerability.

Addressing the conceptual confusion is important and timely since AMLO won the presidency with more than 50% of the vote, which provides him with a clear mandate for change as well as significant legitimacy, and thus the opportunity to reform Mexico's security structures. This discussion is also relevant because misconceptions do not allow for the formulation of efficient public policies, nor for the possibility for the state to identify the most adequate tools at its disposal to confront an intricate security environment.

The central argument of this analysis holds that in the absence of a clear distinction among national security and other designations such as "internal" and "public", essential to an ordered process to reorganize security policy in Mexico, the measures the current or future administrations implement to combat insecurity will not be effective. A clear comprehension of the labels attached to the concept of security is a fundamental precondition to correctly identifying the challenges and, consequently, the instruments to deal with them. The government needs to understand this distinction and intelligence as an essential instrument of the state – not necessarily as a political control mechanism – in order to resort to the correct tools in its toolbox. The AMLO administration is concerned with reversing the relationship between coercive and non-coercive measures to deal with insecurity by emphasizing a social approach, but that might not be enough to succeed without effective police and judicial reform to end impunity in the country, even though steps have already been taken in this direction regarding state and municipal police forces (Gobierno de Mexico 2019).

Confusion about the concept of national security has the potential to aggravate the situation internally, not only because militarization of public security has contributed to violations of human rights and to the exposure of the armed forces to corruption without stemming drug-violence, but also because, by lacking a clear grasp of the nature of the concept, the country has become more vulnerable by neglecting the domestic impact of regional and global developments.

There is an evident and serious paradox: while it is clear that the government still holds a preeminently inward-looking view of security, the country is also becoming more exposed to the international environment. At the end of 2019, for instance, the migrant caravans from Central America, on the one hand, and US pressure on Mexico to secure its southern border (Frederick 2019), on the other, represented just an example of how a combination of factors originating beyond its borders has an impact on Mexico's national security in terms of sovereignty and territorial integrity. Furthermore, AMLO's statement that "the drug war is over" and that security forces will no longer go after drug kingpins in the country (Quackenbush 2019) is also casting a potential conflict with the United States – on top of the marijuana and opium poppy legalization proposal – at a time of increasing traffic of fentanyl coming from Mexico (Diaz-Roman 2020). Moreover, Mexico's Secretary of Foreign Affairs (SRE) made official Mexico's candidacy to one of the non-permanent seats at the UN Security Council for the 2021–2022 period at the 74th Session of the UN General Assembly on September 28, 2019, without an apparent strategy for the country to confront the potential challenges that usually accrue to this position, such as the pressure to side with the United States in detriment of Mexico's limited margin of maneuver provided by its foreign policy principles, as it occurred in 2003 in reference to the US invasion of Iraq, which Mexico finally did not support (AFP 2010).

It is in this context that the purpose of this study is to explain the origin of the confusion in Mexico regarding the distinction among national, internal, and public security. This explanation is intended to be the basis of a new perspective that will contribute to the formulation of a national security policy better equipped to deal with the country's challenges, both domestic and foreign, and to the identification of the most adequate instruments to confront these, often, interconnected issues. This does not mean that Mexico's domestic challenges are unimportant; it rather means that they are not reason enough to neglect the impact of the external environment on Mexico's national security.

Chapter 1 explains that national security is a subfield of IR by having a basic external dimension and, as such, that it is unique and distinct from the concepts of internal and public security. It specifically addresses the realist, "traditional", security perspective in order to understand the origin of the "national" label attached to security, without delving into the broader debate surrounding the widening of the concept of security, which is beyond the scope of this analysis. It also provides a conceptual distinction among national, internal, and public security.

Chapter 2 identifies the origin of the conceptual distortion in Mexico based on the fact that national security is a relatively new subject in the country, and explains the elements that are at the core of the Mexican perspective. It also deals with the unfinished transition of the concept, from an inward-looking view toward a more traditional conceptualization, as it has failed to fully incorporate the broader impact of external factors into public policy, beyond the usual concern about the potential for the United States to influence Mexican affairs.

Chapter 3 reviews the national security notion as it has evolved through the official six-year-term National Development Plans (PND) and National Security Programs. It also addresses the conceptual confusion present in Mexico's 2005 National Security Law (LSN).

After answering *who* defines national security, Chapter 4 focuses on *how* the concept is implemented. It describes the security structures and policies developed within the framework of the current understanding of national security, and the second conceptual confusion created by drug trafficking, as this phenomenon gradually moved from a public security context to become a national security threat, in the process of mixing the instruments available to the state to confront this challenge.

Chapter 5 deals with Mexico's domestic and foreign security contexts, and therefore with the need to reconfigure the national security paradigm based on their interplay. The discussion revisits the argument that the country requires an understanding of national security to correctly identifying threats as well as the most adequate means to confront them, in terms of a more dynamic domestic situation and a more complex security environment. Improving security conditions in Mexico lies in understanding the concept of national security in order to generate a positive change. This task cannot be postponed.

Bibliography

Agence France-Presse (AFP). (November 10, 2010). "Bush: Fox Rehuyo Dialogo sobre la Resolución para Invadir Irak". *La Jornada*. Retrieved from: https://www.jornada.com.mx/2010/11/10/politica/021n1pol

Cerda-Ardura, A. (October 11, 2011). "Los Matazetas, Apuesta por Mayor Violencia". Entrevista a Luis Astorga Almanza/Investigador del Instituto de Investigaciones Sociales de la UNAM. *Siempre!* Retrieved from: http://www.siempre.com.mx/2011/10/los-matazetas-apuesta-por-mayor-violencia/

Diaz-Roman, M. P. (March 16, 2020). "La Crisis de Fentanilo en Estados Unidos Amenaza a México". *Animal Politico*. Retrieved from: https://www.animalpolitico.com/seguridad-180/la-crisis-de-fentanilo-en-estados-unidos-amenaza-a-mexico/

Felbab-Brown, V. (March, 2019). *AMLO's Security Policy: Creative Ideas, Though Reality*. The Brookings Institution. Retrieved from: https://www.brookings.edu/wp-content/uploads/2019/03/FP_20190325_mexico_anti-crime.pdf

Felbab-Brown, V. (September, 2013). "Despite Its Siren Song, High-Value Targeting Doesn't Fit All: Matching Interdiction Patterns to Specific Narcoterrorism and Organized-crime Contexts". *The Brookings Institution*. Paper Delivered at the Counter Narco-Terrorism and Drug Interdiction Conference in Miami September 16–19, 2013. Washington, DC: The Brookings Institution. Retrieved from: https://www.brookings.edu/wp-content/uploads/2016/06/FelbabBrown-Matching-Interdiction-Patterns-to-Specific-Threat-Environments.pdf

Frederick, J. (July 13, 2019). "How Mexico Beefs Up Immigration Enforcement to Meet Trump's Terms". *National Public Radio* (NPR). Retrieved from: https://www.npr.org/2019/07/13/740009105/how-mexico-beefs-up-immigration-enforcement-to-meet-trumps-terms

Gobierno de Mexico. (November 1, 2019). *Construir y Fortalecer a las Policías Estatales y Municipales Desde Abajo, Elementos Clave Para la Recuperación de la Paz: Alfonso Durazo*. Secretaria de Seguridad y Proteccion Ciudadana (SSPC). Retrieved from: https://www.gob.mx/sspc/prensa/construir-y-fortalecer-a-las-policias-estatales-y-municipales-desde-abajo-elementos-clave-para-la-recuperacion-de-la-paz-alfonso-durazo

Maciel, A. (2002). *La Seguridad Nacional. Concepto y Evolucion en Mexico*. San Luis Potosi: El Colegio de San Luis, A.C.

Migueles, R. (July 26, 2019). "INEGI: Sexenio de Peña Nieto Rompe Record en Homicidios". *El Universal*. Retrieved from: https://www.eluniversal.com.mx/nacion/sociedad/inegi-sexenio-de-pena-nieto-rompe-record-en-homicidios

"Plataforma México. Simplemente un mito?" (2018, December 19). *El Universal*. Retrieved from: https://www.eluniversal.com.mx/observatorio-nacional-ciudadano/plataforma-mexico-simplemente-un-mito

Quackenbush, C. (January 13, 2019). "There Is Officially No More War. Mexico's President Declares an End to the Drug War Amid Skepticism". *TIME*. Retrieved from: https://time.com/5517391/mexico-president-ends-drug-war/

Redaccion. (July 5, 2018). "Cisen Desaparecera, Ejercito Regresara a Cuarteles y Segob Dejara de Ser 'Un Monstruo Ingobernable': Alfonso Durazo". *Aristegui Noticias*. Retrieved from: https://aristeguinoticias.com/0507/mexico/cisen-desaparecera-ejercito-regresara-a-cuarteles-y-segob-dejara-de-ser-un-monstruo-ingobernable-alfonso-durazo/

Redaccion. (November 29, 2019a). "4 Graficas que Miden el Primer Año de AMLO como Presidente". *El Financiero*. Retrieved from: https://www.elfinanciero.com.mx/nacional/4-graficas-que-miden-el-primer-ano-de-amlo-como-presidente

Redaccion. (December 11, 2019b). "Diputados Aprueban en lo General la Ley de Amnistia; Es Más Populismo que Justicia, Acusa el PAN". *Animal Politico*. Retrieved from: https://www.animalpolitico.com/2019/12/diputados-aprueban-ley-amnistia/

1 National Security and Its External Dimension

1.1 Security as a Relative Concept

This chapter addresses national security as a key concept of political realism, a dominant IR school of thought that emphasizes the central role of the state and military power in the international system. The point of this discussion is not to debate or reject its explanatory limitations, but to identify its origin as inextricably linked to the exterior and, therefore, to underline its inadequacy to describe internal security challenges. Nevertheless, this is what actually occurs in Mexico as the concept of national security is often used in reference to issues that can be best described as either internal of public security challenges.

Security is a political concept that, by its ambiguity, has lent itself to different interpretations, often to legitimize the power of the state to implement extraordinary measures to confront existential threats. This is the outcome of what Buzan et al. identify as the "securitization" process (Buzan, Waever and de Wilde 1998: 25).

While most characterizations of security comprise elements such as actors, goals, obstacles, and dynamics, defining a generally accepted concept is problematic because security is contextual and dependent on the circumstances. For Colombia, for instance, having US military advisors within its territory as part of "Plan Colombia" is less of a security concern, in comparison to the presence of US military personnel stationed in Mexico as part of the "Merida Initiative", which the Mexican government rejected because of the historic distrust of US intentions (Petras 2000/2001). A relevant recommendation from contrasting each country's posture suggests Mexico to:

> Increase policymakers' willingness to accept international support, especially from the United States. The United States can be immensely helpful in training and equipping Mexican forces and

> mentoring Mexican police in intelligence-gathering tactics, techniques, and procedures.
>
> (Paul, Clark and Serena 2014: 92)

Even though this study emphasizes the difficulties involved in defining a generally accepted concept, it does recognize that there are basic elements that underpin the idea of security. First, security is about "values" that as such require to be protected from threats (Wolfers 1952: 484). Second, security is basically the "pursuit of freedom from threat" (Buzan 1991: 18). That is, it is defined by a "negative value" in the sense that it is characterized by the absence of a threat, resembling the debates about "positive" and "negative" freedom in political philosophy (see Berlin 1969). Third, security represents a cost, which means that resources devoted to security do so at the expense of satisfying other needs in a context of "scarce resources" (Baldwin 1997: 14–5). However, allocating resources to security implies not only a trade-off regarding other goals, but also the possibility of creating a "security dilemma" by making others feel less secure because of one's own actions, diminishing, in turn, one's own security (see Herz 1951). Fourth, security is relative because it often implies accepting a minimum level of insecurity, depending on the threat perception. According to a 1950s classic essay,

> Some may find the danger to which they are exposed entirely normal and in line with their modest security expectations while others consider it unbearable to live with these same dangers.
>
> (Wolfers 1952: 485–6)

Security, therefore, is an issue related to perception, in line with the constructivist view on the subject that establishes that the concept is inter-subjective and socially constructed (see Katzenstein 1996). Because of its ambiguity, security is a notion that cannot be defined in absolute terms, but only in reference to specific contexts.

1.2 Realist Perspective

If it is true that there is a wide variety of definitions of national security in the literature on the subject, this concept is at the basis of National Security Studies that, in turn, is a sub-field of IR. Notwithstanding the relativity of security, "national security" unequivocally refers first, and foremost, to the state and relations of power (military) vis-à-vis other states in the international system. This notion is based on a set of principles as established by political realism, one of the most influential IR theories.

National security is about both defending and promoting the national interest, which is the concrete expression of values and aspirations. According to Nuechterlein, "the *national interest* is the perceived needs and desires of one sovereign state in relation to the sovereign states comprising its external environment" (1978: 3). This is actually the key to understand the nature of security when the "national" label is attached to it, and the principle often neglected in Mexico.

The traditional notion of national security and its focus on the state and military factors has its roots in "classical realism" and "neorealism" within IR theory. Realism has been a dominant perspective whose antecedents can be traced back to a specific school of thought (Thucydides 1951; Hobbes 1954; Machiavelli 1981), which in the 20th Century represented a criticism of the "utopianism" of the interwar period. In his book *The Twenty Years Crisis, 1919–1939* published in 1939, for instance, Carr rejected a "natural harmony of interests" in the international system, by considering it the source of "so much confusion in international thinking" (1995: 50).

Morgenthau, the leading proponent of this view after WWII, in his *Politics Among Nations*, criticized "the 'legalistic-moralistic approach' to international politics" (1993: 14). He established that the world "is the result of forces inherent in the human nature", one of "opposing interests and of conflict" where there is no place for morality, especially if it is defined in isolation from reality (1993: 3). His perspective on international politics is based on a set of principles that emphasize that international politics is about "interest defined in terms of power", and the permanence of the state as a crucial "moral principle" (1993: 4–14). States are rational and unitary actors operating in an anarchic international system, seeking to maximize their power to promote their national interests through use of the force. This is why power, meaning military power, equals security within this perspective, which, in turn, has been the basis of Strategic Studies as an interdisciplinary academic field. Furthermore, in a competitive international context of sovereign states, balance of power represents "a particular manifestation of a general social principle" that is fundamental to preserve states' freedom of action (1993: 183).

In contrast to classical realism, for neo-realism or "structural realism", understanding international politics requires focusing not on the human nature, but on the nature of the international system; the system, in turn, comprises a "structure" and "interactive units" (Waltz 1979: 79). While the structure is defined by the way each unit is related to all others, units are states that are differentiated not by the objectives they seek to accomplish, but by the array of instruments at their disposal to achieve their goals (Waltz 1979: 80 and 97). The theory's most important variables are located at the system level, not at the level of the unit, and this is actually a source of criticism made of realism and neo-realism as well, for failing to consider the internal characteristics of individual units, which otherwise would provide valuable elements of analysis:

> The proposition that the state might be essentially problematic or contested is excluded from neorealist theory. Indeed, neorealist theory is prepared to acknowledge problems of the state only to the extent that the state itself, within the framework of its own legitimations, might be prepared to recognize problems and mobilize resources toward their solution.
>
> (Ashley 1986: 269)

In comparison to the hierarchical nature of domestic politics, where there is a vertical line of authority, the defining principle of international politics is *anarchy*, which is created by each unit looking for its own self-serving interest (Waltz 1979: 88). As a result of this "self-help" principle, the primary goal of states is "survival" (Waltz 1979: 91). As in classical realism, balance of power is a relevant concept, even though within neo-realism it is a circumstance defined by both the anarchic structure and the units' search for their survival (Waltz 1979: 121). This means that for every change in the structure, there is a corresponding alteration of the units' posture in the international system.

One significant criticism of the realist school comes from pluralism, in particular from the neo-liberal institutionalist strand and its concept of "complex interdependence". This view establishes that in the international context, societies are inter-connected by a wide range of links; that military issues are not at the top of the state's agenda; and that military power is increasingly difficult to translate into other forms of influence (Keohane and Nye 1989: 21–2). Even though this perspective does not reject the relevance of the state and military factors, it challenges the claim about them being the decisive aspects of international politics. One interdependence line of argument found in one of the texts of the Copenhagen School, for instance, is that "in the post-Cold War world, a case can be made that military threats are ceasing to matter in relations among the advanced industrial democracies" (Buzan, Waever and de Wilde 1998: 62). One example of this is the Franco-German brigade established in 1987, which is evidence of a collaborative security arrangement after centuries of rivalry (Von Wolff Metternicht 1991).

Realism, neo-realism, and neo-liberalism are all positivist perspectives, which means that they describe phenomena that are observable and measurable, also known as "empiricism" (Markie 2017). From the post-positivist side – that rejects the principles of positivism by establishing that observation is fallible and theory susceptible to correction – the realist/neo-realist perspective is also criticized by the "English School" which, contrary to realism, holds that states can actually abide by rules that contribute to sustain "common interests", and by doing so they create a "society of states" meaning that anarchy does not necessarily translate into conflict (Bull 2002: 13). One of the outstanding criticisms of realism/neo-realism is its failure to satisfactorily explain the causes of war. According to Jervis, a realist himself, making reference to the international context after the end of the Cold War,

> Whatever its explanation, the very existence of a security community among the leading powers refutes many theories of the causes of war or, at least, indicates they are not universally valid.
>
> (Jervis 2002: 11)

Among additional theoretical views that are also critical of positivist/rational choice theory approaches, Critical Theory challenges the epistemological basis of realism (i.e. the state of nature and states as rational actors) to provide an alternative perspective based on the idea of "emancipation", and thus the rejection of the *status quo* in the international system as promoted by realism, which is considered an approach maintaining prevailing power relations.

At the core of Critical Security Studies (CSS) is its refutation of the "state-centric character" of realism, and the fact that states "can be a source of insecurity themselves", which requires therefore to emphasize the "individual" and the "communities" as the "main referent objects of security" (Booth 1991: 319–20). CSS, in turn, is criticized in terms of a controversial notion such as emancipation (i.e. the freeing of people) because it could be "appropriated for neo-imperialistic" objectives to impose Western views on non-Western peoples, such as in the case of humanitarian interventions (Olivares 2018).

Realism, therefore, has explanatory limitations and it has been criticized in terms of both its depth and width to understand security by pointing to the need of considering additional actors besides the states and "sectors" besides the military one (see Buzan, Waever and de Wilde 1998). However, both aspects continue as "fundamental referents" in the contemporary world and, hence, realism and its national security by-product maintain a prominent role in understanding the international system. As a matter of fact, there is no contradiction for national security, as a byproduct of realism, to consider in principle additional referent objects besides the state and sectors besides the military one, as security analysis cannot be completely separated from realist principles. For instance, making reference to its own analysis, those in favor of widening the concept of national security such as Buzan, Weaver and de Wilde establish that,

> The main purpose of [*Security: A New Framework for Analysis*] is to present a framework based on the wider agenda that will incorporate the traditionalist [realist] position. Our solution comes down to the side of the wideners in terms of keeping the security agenda open to many different types of threats.
>
> (Buzan, Waever and de Wilde 1998: 4).

Incorporating the "traditionalist position" means that using the term "national security" to refer to domestic security challenges is misleading, especially when they are unrelated to the external world.

It is possible to argue that national security is a concept that best describes competition among strong states, great power-type of challenges, and less suited to explain the predicament of weak, developing countries. According to Ayoob, security in developing nations is characterized more by the "twin tasks of state making and state building", than by external concerns. The challenges faced by developing states, therefore, are better conceptualized as internal security concerns (1991: 281). In Mexico, for instance, it is correct to categorize drug trafficking as a "national security" issue, not only because it affects each one of the components of the state, evident, for instance, in the weakness of its institutions in the face of the corrupting power of organized crime, but more importantly because it is a threat originating in the international system. Otherwise, if drug trafficking only affected the components of the state without any links to the exterior, it would be better described as an internal security matter to be addressed primarily by social, economic, law enforcement measures, keeping the armed forces, a national security instrument *par excellence*, on the sidelines, and not as a permanent response. This rationale intends to address the existing confusion of terms in Mexico, as it will be discussed below.

1.3 Different Labels, Different Contexts

In contrast to the state's concerns regarding the international environment, which fall within the national security realm, internal security is about events occurring within the borders of a state, and they are usually related to maintaining internal order and protecting the citizenry (Torchio 2018). In comparison to the military that is primarily responsible for national security by upholding sovereignty and territorial integrity, internal security is the purview of security forces such as the police and paramilitary units and, only in exceptional cases, of the military itself (Soto-Morales 2017).

The fact that national security and internal security are different does not mean that they are not connected, as internal security threats, such as civil disorder, large-scale violence, armed insurgency, or domestic terrorism, can turn into a threat to the population, institutions, or infrastructure, thus requiring the temporary intervention of the armed forces when civilian security forces are insufficient to deal with the intensity of the threat.

In contrast to the United States where there are strict *Posse Comitatus* limitations on the use of the armed forces for domestic security purposes (Maciel 2019), most democratic countries are less reticent to use the military within their borders, even though they recognize the primacy of the civilian leadership over the military. For instance, in France, the *Gendarmerie Nationale*, which was borne as part of the armed forces, is employed for domestic purposes; it is made up of both military and civilian units, and since 2009 was placed under the Ministry of the Interior (CESOP 2019: 22).

In this context,

> the flexibility of the distinction and the possibility of the intervention of the armed forces in matters considered in the first instance of internal security could be considered, in these particular cases, a question of practicality rather than a philosophical matter.
>
> (Torchio 2018)

In any case, the participation of the military in domestic affairs has to be an exception, not the rule, because the primary responsibility of the armed forces is external defense. It has been argued that involving the military in domestic security issues, and especially in confronting the new "asymmetric threats", is a formula both to provide them with a new mission and an opportunity for the governments to rein in their budgets, which at the end means degrading and converting them in subsidiaries of the security forces (Torchio 2018), which is contrary to the tenets of political realism.

Regarding public security, this is a function of governments focusing on protecting the integrity, interests, and property of the people. It is about preserving public order through prevention, investigation, and prosecution of crimes that constitute a threat to the well-being and the prosperity of the communities (Mendoza 2017). While national security is an issue that corresponds to the armed forces, public security is a matter for law enforcement organizations to deal with, more generally at the municipal level, while national security is a federal matter.

In the case of Mexico, there is an enduring confusion about the distinction among national, internal, and public security, both in terms of objectives and instruments. Comparing national and public security, for instance, while the objective of the former is to preserve the country's national interests as established in the LSN (Camara de Diputados 2019: 1–2b), the latter is to protect the integrity and rights of the citizens, according to the General Law of the National System of Public Security (Camara de Diputados 2019: 1a). While national security matters are a federal affair, public security is a concurrent matter, meaning that it requires the joint participation of the federal, state, and municipal levels.

The source of the conceptual confusion regarding national and public security is the law itself. For instance, the President has a leading role in both national security and public security matters in this latter case by presiding over the National Council for Public Security as established by legislation (Camara de Diputados 2019: 5a). A similar confusion is evident in the fact that in Mexico, also by law, national security includes internal security, as it will be discussed in more detail below.

For the sake of greater clarity, therefore, it is important to consider threats to internal order as national security matters only to the extent they are related to developments abroad; otherwise, they should be considered internal security issues in order to establish a distinction between "national" and "internal" to prevent the concept of national security from losing its coherence and utility.

Bibliography

Ashley, R. K. (1986). "The Poverty of Neorealism". In R. O. Keohane (Ed.), *Neorealism and Its Critics*. New Directions in World Politics. Helen Milner and John Gerard Ruggie, General Editors (p. 269). New York, NY: Columbia University Press.

Ayoob, M. (1991). "The Security Problematic of the Third World". *World Politics*. Vol. 43. Retrieved from: https://www.researchgate.net/publication/259380013_The_Security_Problematic_of_the_Third_World

Baldwin, D. A. (January, 1997). "The Concept of Security". *Review of International Studies*, Vol. 23, No. 1, 14, 15.

Berlin, I. (1969). "Two Concepts of Liberty". In I. Berlin, *Four Essays on Liberty*. London: Oxford University Press. In Hardy, H. (Ed.). (2002). *Liberty* (New Ed.). Oxford: Oxford University Press. Stanford Encyclopedia of Philosophy, *Positive and Negative Liberty*, October 8, 2007. Retrieved from: http://plato.stanford.edu/entries/liberty-positive-negative/

Booth, K. (1991). "Security and Emancipation". *Review of International Studies*. Vol. 17. Retrieved from: https://www.jstor.org/stable/20097269 [Accessed 22 October 2017].

Bull, H. (2002). *The Anarchical Society. A Study of Order in World Politics*. Third Edition, with Forewords by Andrew Hurrell and Stanley Hoffman. Basingstoke: Palgrave.

Buzan, B. (1991). *People, States, and Fear: An Agenda for International Security Studies in the Post-Cold War Era* (2nd Ed.). Hertfordshire: Harvester Wheatsheaf.

Buzan, B., Waever, O., and de Wilde, J. (1998). *Security: A New Framework for Analysis*. Boulder, CO: Lynne Rienner Publishers.

Camara de Diputados del H. Congreso de la Union. (May 27, 2019a). *Ley General del Sistema Nacional de Seguridad Publica*. Nueva Ley publicada en el Diario Oficial de la Federacion el 2 de enero de 2009. Retrieved from: http://www.diputados.gob.mx/LeyesBiblio/pdf/LGSNSP_270519.pdf

Camara de Diputados del H. Congreso de la Union. (November 8, 2019b). *Ley de Seguridad Nacional*. Nueva Ley publicada en el Diario Oficial de la Federacion el 31 de enero de 2005. Retrieved from: http://www.diputados.gob.mx/LeyesBiblio/pdf/LSegNac_081119.pdf

Carr, E. H. (1995). *The Twenty Years' Crisis, 1919–1939*. London: Papermac.

Centro de Estudios Sociales y de Opinión Pública (CESOP). (March, 2019). *La Guardia Nacional. Carpeta Informativa*. Gobierno Constitucional del Estado de Oaxaca. Poder Legislativo. LXIV Legislatura.

Herz, J. H. (1951). *Political Realism and Political Idealism: A Study in Theories and Realities*. Chicago, IL: University of Chicago Press.

Hobbes, T. (1954). *Leviathan*. Edited by Michael Oakeshott. New York, NY: Collier Macmillan.

Jervis, R. (March, 2002). "Theories of War and Peace in an Era of Leading-Power Peace. 'Presidential Address, American Political Science Association, 2001'". *The American Political Science Review*. Vol. 96, No. 1, 11.

Katzenstein, P. J. (1996). *The Culture of National Security: Norms and Identity in World Politics*. New York, NY: Columbia University Press.

Keohane, R. O., and Nye, J. S. (1989). *Power and Interdependence* (2nd Ed.). Written under the auspices of the Center for International Affairs, Harvard University. New York, NY: HarperCollins Publishers.

Machiavelli, N. (1981). *The Prince*. Translated with an introduction by George Bull. Penguin Classics. London: Penguin Books.

Maciel, A. (2019). "Cuando la tradicion no es un lujo, sino un imperativo: Lecciones del caso estadounidense para la militarizacion de la seguridad publica en Mexico". In M. P. Moloeznik and I. Medina Nuñez (Eds.), "Proceso de Militarizacion de la Seguridad Publica en America Latina". *Contextualizaciones Latinoamericanas* (pp. 237–271). Guadalajara: Universidad de Guadalajara.

Markie, P. (Fall, 2017 Ed.). "Rationalism vs. Empiricism". *The Stanford Encyclopedia of Philosophy.* In E. N. Zalta (Ed.). Retrieved from: https://plato.stanford.edu/archives/fall2017/entries/rationalism-empiricism/

Mendoza, A. (March 18, 2017). "Definicion de la Seguridad Publica". *Enciclopedia Juridica Mexicana.* Retrieved from: https://mexico.leyderecho.org/definicion-de-la-seguridad-publica/

Morgenthau, H. J. (1993). *Politics among Nations. The Struggle for Power and Peace* (Brief Ed.). Revised by K. W. Thompson. New York, NY: McGraw-Hill.

Nuechterlein, D. E. (1978). *National Interest and Presidential Leadership,* Westview Special Studies in International Relations. Boulder, CO: Westview Press.

Olivares, M. (May 2, 2018). "Has Critical Security Studies Run Out of Steam?" University of Westminster. Retrieved from: https://www.e-ir.info/2018/05/02/has-critical-security-studies-run-out-of-steam/

Paul, C., Clarke, C. P., and Serena, C. C. (2014). *Mexico Is Not Colombia. Alternative Historical Analogies for Responding to the Challenge of Violent Drug-Trafficking Organizations.* International Security and Defense Policy Center at National Security Research Division. Santa Monica, CA: RAND Corporation.

Petras, J. (December 30, 2000–January 5, 2001). "Geopolitics of Plan Colombia". *Economic and Political Weekly.* Vol. 35, No. 52/53, 4617–4623.

Soto-Morales, R. (June 5, 2017). "Seguridad Interior". *Infodefensa.com.* Retrieved from: https://www.infodefensa.com/latam/2017/06/05/opinion-seguridad-interior.php

Thucydides. (1951). *The Peloponnesian War.* Translated by John H. Finley, Jr. New York, NY: Modern Library.

Torchio, G. (June 3, 2018). "Defensa Nacional-Seguridad Interior. A Cerca del Nuevo Rol de las Fuerzas Armadas". *La Señal Medios.* Retrieved from: https://xn--lasealmedios-dhb.com.ar/2018/06/03/defensa-nacional-seguridad-interior-acerca-del-nuevo-rol-de-las-fuerzas-armadas/

Von Wolff Metternich, D. (1991). "The Franco-German Brigade: A German Perspective". *The RUSI Journal.* Vol. 136, No. 3. Retrieved from: https://www.tandfonline.com/doi/abs/10.1080/03071849108445534?journalCode=rusi20

Waltz, K. N. (1979). *Theory of International Politics.* New York, NY: McGraw-Hill.

Wolfers, A. (December, 1952). "National Security as an Ambiguous Symbol". *Political Science Quarterly.* Vol. 61, No. 4, 485–486.

2 Obstacles to Understanding National Security in Mexico

2.1 An Underdeveloped Notion

This chapter explains that addressing national security is a matter of just a few decades in Mexico, whose discussion was delayed by both the discredit of the concept in South America during the Cold War and the need prevent the United States from identifying its security interests with those of its neighbor to the south, under a dominant nationalist ideology. The country has a predominantly inward-looking "national security" perspective explained by both its geopolitical situation and the demilitarization of its political system. The opening of its economy since the mid-1980s and a closer economic relationship with the United States, nevertheless, have increasingly exposed the country to developments beyond its borders and, therefore, it needs to adapt its national security perspective accordingly.

National security has not been a central issue in political debates in Mexico and its discussion, although gradually increasing since the 1980s, does not reflect a long-standing tradition. The subject has not been dominant in the country's politics because of the negative connotation of the concept in the Southern Cone in the context of the Cold War, when military regimes justified repression of political opposition under the logic of an "internal enemy" (Leal-Buitrago 2003). This is what in Latin America became known as the "National Security Doctrine".

Politicians in Mexico also avoided public discussion of the issue out of concern for the possibility for the United States to identify common interests in the resulting Mexican definition, thus opening the door to US intervention, a closer relationship, and conflict (Bailey and Shelton-Colby 1992: 2).

Among the variety of definitions found in the Mexican literature on the subject, one of them establishes that national security is,

> The set of conditions -political, economic, military, social and cultural- required to guarantee the sovereignty, the independence

> and the promotion of the nation's interest, strengthening the national project components and reducing to the minimum the weaknesses or inconsistencies that could translate themselves in vulnerability windows vis-à-vis the external environment.
>
> (Herrera-Lasso and Gonzalez 1990: 391)

This non-official definition is interesting because it emphasizes the importance of the "external environment" in line with the traditional concept, in comparison to a wide variety of others that overlook this point. One of the official definitions in Mexico is found in the LSN:

> For the purposes of this Law, National Security means actions aimed immediately and directly to maintain the integrity, stability and permanence of the Mexican State, which lead to: the protection of the Mexican nation against threats and risks faced by our country; the preservation of national sovereignty and independence and the defense of the territory; the maintenance of constitutional order and the strengthening of democratic institutions of government; the maintenance of the unity of the integral parts of the Federation designated in article 43 of the Political Constitution of the United Mexican States; the legitimate defense of the Mexican State with respect to other States or subjects of international law; and the preservation of democracy, founded on the social and political economic development of the country and its inhabitants.
>
> (Camara de Diputados 2019b)

In comparison to the non-official definition, the law defines national security in terms of *actions* rather than *conditions*, which does not make sense, as the basis of national security is values translated into concrete interests. Furthermore, the law defines threats rather than permanent national interests, which is an error considering that threats are dynamic rather than constant, transforming themselves with changes in the security environment.

This particular conceptualization found in the LSN suggests that internal security is embedded in national security, by "maintaining the constitutional order" as a referent object of national security. If it is true that the official definition takes into consideration domestic and external factors, in Mexico discourse has not translated into policy, as national security, for all practical purposes, has been dominated by an inward-looking perspective and the need to deal with drug-related violence. In this context, the term is loosely used to refer to challenges that more often fall within the area of either internal or public security, and examples of this abound in public opinion, both in written and oral statements. Mexico, therefore, not only came late to the discussion of its national security but also, when the issue was finally addressed, this occurred without the proper understanding to do so.

There are several reasons why the national security concept in Mexico has not reflected the traditional realist perspective (i.e. concern for foreign military threats), and they are related to its geopolitical situation and the nature of its political system. Its main preoccupation related to the external environment has historically been dominated, directly and indirectly, by the United States, in the process overlooking other international issues and areas of the world to which Mexico is also increasingly exposed.

2.2 Elements of Its *Sui-generis* View

Mexico's national security notion has long been based on objectives such as the defense of national sovereignty and the preservation of internal stability through political, economic, and social means. Even though the government has resorted to repression in the past – such as in the 1959 railroad workers strike, the 1968 student movement, and the "dirty war" of the 1970s – the country's stability was maintained by the political system's corporatist structure and its ability, under the PRI, to co-opt and to incorporate the demands of the different sectors of society (Editors 2018).

Mexico's inward-looking national security perspective, current throughout the post-revolutionary period to the present day, is explained by two factors: its geopolitical situation and the nature of its political system, in particular the de-politicization of the military and the stability achieved by the civilian leadership.

Geopolitics

Mexico has a peculiar geopolitical situation: it is flanked by the Gulf of Mexico and the Caribbean to the East, and the Pacific Ocean to the West; to the north, it shares a 3,000 km border with a superpower, and to the south, land, fluvial, and maritime boundaries with two Central American countries (Guatemala and Belize) with limited military capabilities. In this context, Mexico's concerns at its borders are of a non-conventional, trans-national, character, as reflected in the illegal flow of people, drugs, arms, and currency.

Its geographical location has traditionally been a concern because of its proximity to the United States. Yet, this situation has also provided Mexico the advantage of having a limited defense budget because it has made no sense either investing significant resources to defend itself against a major nuclear power, or from countries not representing a substantial military threat. Historically, Mexican defense spending has been one of the lowest in Latin America as a GDP percentage. While in 2018 the regional average was 1.3%, for Mexico, it was 0.5% (World Bank 2019). Mexican armed forces are also modest in relation to the country's territory and population size, as well as in terms of its economy. With a similar population size (127 million people), for instance, Mexico's military spending is less than that of Japan (126 million people), a country with close security ties with the United States that devotes 0.9% to its Self-Defense Forces (World Bank 2019).

The limited size of its military has also been related to the fact that the government does not consider it a fundamental factor of its foreign policy (Dziedzic 1985: 114). Defense of the Mexican territory has been implicitly guaranteed by the United States because of the country's strategic position on the US southern flank:

> Mexico automatically falls within the security umbrella of its northern neighbor since an assault on its territory would undoubtedly be treated as a precursor to attack on the United States itself. Mexico consequently enjoys the benefits of a de facto alliance without its attendant obligations. This, coupled with a dearth of serious external threats, has historically liberated Mexico's defense planners from preoccupation with its international environment.
>
> (Dziedzic 1985: 111)

Even though the aforementioned argument is essentially correct, the main foreign threat to Mexico has historically been the United States itself. The US-Mexico strategic relationship, therefore, is a two-way road where Mexico also represents an advantage to US security as a "pivot State", whose collapse or progress is key to regional stability (Chase, Hill and Kennedy 1996: 37).

Having the United States as the implicit guarantor of its external security has allowed Mexico to focus on its domestic security challenges, and this is a factor that in part explains its preeminent inward-looking security perspective. Nevertheless, the impact of external developments on Mexico does not exclusively originate in the United States, and this is a fact the government is obliged to come to terms with.

Political System

Besides geography, a determinant of national security in Mexico has been the limited participation of the armed forces both in the definition of the concept and the decision about the means to confront threats, as they have been "essentially passive on foreign defense matters" (Merrill and Miro 1997: 281).

The Mexican Revolution (1910–1921) and its aftermath were characterized by violent competition for power among *caudillos*. Since the 1920s, nevertheless, civilian leaders were able to separate the military from politics: they resorted to the frequent rotation of military zone commanders (to prevent the development of personal loyalties either by the troops or local politicians); to the provision of "generous material incentives" short of accumulating excessive power to challenge the civilian leadership; and required from those in the ranks who were interested in politics, to participate in their personal capacity, not as representatives of their institution (Cornelius 1996: 85). They were also given control of the intelligence apparatus as a compensation for their lack of political participation (see Navarro 2010).

Toward the end of the 1940s, Mexico already had a demilitarized political system. The political activity of its high ranks had been restricted to non-violent competition and negotiation, within the institutionalized decision-making framework dominated by the civilian leadership. In this context, from the end of the 1940s, after Manuel Avila-Camacho's presidential term (1940–1946) – the last President to come from the military – the Army was firmly under the control of the civilian apparatus of the state (Grayson 1999: 6).

Because it has been defined by the civilian leadership, national security in Mexico has not been about risk of aggression; instead, it has been related to the achievement of goals such as social justice, economic development, and the defense of sovereignty, as established in the 1917 Constitution (Pellicer 1983: 188), which contributed to promote stability. According to a view, this stability is what actually distinguished Mexico from other countries in the region:

> In the majority of Latin American political systems, the 'distance' between crisis, instability and coup d'état is minimal. Mexico is different: over and over its political system has demonstrated a deep capacity to absorb conflict and internal crises without becoming unstable.
>
> (Ronfeldt 1984: 11)

The absence of concern about the external environment, beyond the United States, has been reflected in both Mexico's foreign and defense policies. Regarding the former, the country's international orientation has for long been essentially defensive, relying on International Law. As a matter of fact, Mexico's foreign policy principles were incorporated in the 1980s in Article 89 of its Constitution (Camara de Diputados 2019: 88a) as a result of policy differences with the United States over armed conflicts in Central America. This posture was the best defense for a weak country, and it made Mexican foreign policy both respectable and predictable in the international arena. It was characterized by a high degree of continuity in what is best described as a "state policy" in contrast to a "government policy", the latter defined by the group in power rather than by long-term national objectives (Gonzalez 1989: 36).

Regarding the latter, the military in Mexico has also had a mission established in the Constitution, and it has been to support internal security and external defense (Camara de Diputados 2019: 88a). The Army, in particular, has three main undertakings (Plan DN-I against an external aggressor; Plan DN-II to respond to internal subversion; Plan DN-III to assist the civilian population in cases of disaster), both of an internal and an external nature, notwithstanding that the latter kind of task has not been the norm (Piñeyro 1995: 7). For instance, the country participates with a very limited group of military officers in UN Peacekeeping operations, notwithstanding Mexico's multilateral activism. According to 2020 figures, the country provides a total of 13 military observers, while a smaller country such as El Salvador, a total of 293 personnel, including 256 troops (UN 2020: 2–4).

Because Mexico has not faced challenges to its territorial integrity since the 19th Century, the country has not been under pressure to develop a traditional defense policy, that is, one oriented toward deterring a specific external aggressor. The gap between the idea of an integral, whole-of-government and society, national defense policy in Mexico, and the reality, is recognized by high-ranking members from the Mexican military postgraduate schools who also consider, as a fundamental first step to build this policy, to clearly define the roles of each and every security institution in the country (Interviews 2020). In the meantime, the fact that Mexican military policy – which is different – has a defensive nature, however, does not mean that the country should not be prepared to confront an uncertain future, either in terms of non-military or military challenges, and this is one of the arguments addressed below.

It is important to note that in the course of the last decades, the participation of the armed forces in the definition of national security in Mexico has been increasing, not only via their membership in both the National Security Cabinet and National Security Council, but also through research and teaching activities carried out by their respective postgraduate schools, and their participation in a wide variety of forums where they exchange ideas with civilian leaders, such as in seminars and conferences, and by interacting with the Mexican Congress (Interviews 2020).

The Mexican Army and Navy's shared definition of national security comprises internal security (SEDENA/SEMAR 2018). This view, nevertheless, is not restricted to the Mexican armed forces as this is also the case in other Latin American militaries, particularly because of the strong 19th-Century Iberic legacy present in the Southern Cone, which justified the intervention of the armed forces in internal politics, and because of the 20th Century's adoption of Franco's Spain military principles (i.e. the obligation of the armed forces to intervene in politics when fundamental aspects of society are at risk), as part of their national security doctrine (Leal-Buitrago 2003: 76–7). This view, nevertheless, lends itself to excesses when it becomes dogmatic (Sanchez and Rodriguez 2006: 123), and this is the reason why it is important to rethink and review the role of the military in society.

2.3 US Factor

The only permanent exception to Mexico's inward-looking "national security" perspective has been the need to react, when possible, to the United States. This country has also been indirectly the reason why Mexico has been compelled to gradually incorporate the impact of other external issues on its outlook, in an unfinished process where its perspective has not yet fully integrated, beyond discourse, the consequences of its broader international exposure.

Historically, US-Mexican relations were characterized either by friction or open conflict from the mid-1800s to the first three decades of the 20th Century. Yet, during WWII, the United States and Mexico became allies and bilateral security co-operation increased to an extent not seen before, or ever since (Paz 1997: 61–73). This collaboration, however, was scaled back after the war, and for all practical purposes their short-term alliance concluded.

For the next three Cold War decades, Mexico had a balanced relationship with the United States. It did not support US military objectives, but it did not become either a security liability for its neighbor. In fact, the rather benign US view toward Mexico at this time was explained not only by its solid political system and adequate economic performance, but also by a satisfactory bilateral interaction (Aguayo 1993: 98).

During the Cold War, Mexico provided an advantage to the United States by keeping the common border free of risks. Because of this benefit, the United States was able to project its military power beyond the hemisphere and into areas of intense geo-strategic competition. Mexico's stability, therefore, "contributed -passively but fundamentally- to the final triumph of the [US] policy of containment" (Dziedzic 1997: 85). Moreover, the two countries have represented a "security community" (Karl Deutch cited by Dziedzic 1989: 4), or a "pluralist security community" (John Muller and Karl Holsti cited by Mares 1996: 41), meaning that military solutions to their disputes are out of the question.

From the US perspective, Mexico has had a tangential military significance, only to the extent that the US military has been required to support law enforcement agencies (LEAs) operating along the US Southwest border, providing them with aerial reconnaissance and ground surveillance capabilities, as well as search and rescue, and medical, support (Garmone 2019). Mexico's only military concern for the United States would be related to the potential of deep instability in the country that could require the US Army to seal the common border. According to Schulz:

> But as important as Brazil, Colombia and Venezuela are to U.S. security interests, they pale beside Mexico. Few countries are more vital to the well-being of the United States than its neighbor to the south. Not only is Mexico our second largest trading partner, but the two countries share a 2,000-mile boundary. Any serious political and economic turmoil below the Rio Grande River [sic] is almost certain to spillover the border in the form of illegal immigrants, political refugees, narcotrafficking, violence and corruption.
>
> (Schulz 1999: 10b)

In the span of the first three decades of the Cold War, interdependence intensified between the two countries, thus expanding the bilateral agenda by increasing its number of issues. Mexico became increasingly relevant in reference to oil, the common border, and the growing impact of each country's domestic politics on the other (The White House 1978: 1).

In contrast to the period of relative stability in US-Mexican relations from the end of WWII to the 1970s, by the 1980s, controversies in the bilateral relationship had become "cumulative" (Whitehead 1991: 245) as a result of a variety of issues, such as the 1977 disagreement over the Mexican trans-border gas pipeline, and Mexico's refusal to let the Shah of Iran to re-enter the country after receiving medical treatment in the United States.

As a matter of fact, "by the end of the 1970s, the relationship that [President Jimmy] Carter had hoped to build with Mexico had become a casualty to miscalculations, divergent perceptions, and some policy differences" (Pastor 1992: 32). More importantly, the growing level of tension between the two countries, even over issues apparently not directly related to the bilateral relationship, such as oil, the Central American armed conflicts and Mexico's 1982 economic crisis proved the Mexican government the relevance of the external environment for the country's national security.

At the end of the 1980s, there was a change in US policies toward Mexico, as explained by the country's economic crises, and uncertainty about its governability and political stability (Aguilar-Camin and Meyer 1993: 225). The significant challenge the left had posed during the previous presidential election in Mexico and the US preference for a PRI government, as well as the almost simultaneous arrival of new administrations in both countries, all these aspects contributed to set the stage for more collaboration by 1989 (Aguilar-Camin and Meyer 1993: 237), paving the way for the 1994 North American Free Trade Agreement (NAFTA).

A detailed examination of the agreement is beyond the scope of this analysis, but it is important to review its security implications for Mexico, as this explains how the country has become more exposed to the international environment.

First of all, it is important to mention that, in general, economic reform in Mexico at the end of the 1980s followed in fact a political rather than an economic rationale:

> The main reason for economic change was political. The outset of the foreign debt crisis in August 1982 seriously threatened the stability of the Mexican political system, and with it the continuing rule of the [Institutional Revolutionary Party] PRI.
>
> (Purcell 1993: 54)

According to this argument, the PRI realized that opening the economy was a condition to retain power. Both the exhaustion of the import substitution industrialization strategy (ISIS) model and political imperatives represented the stimulus for change. In terms of the predictability a regional free trade agreement was thought to provide, a further benefit would consist in locking in liberal reform in Mexico. In this context, US-Mexico free trade had "[grown] out of the desire to set a new structure in place that would be extremely difficult for future [Mexican] governments to reverse" (Weintraub and Baer 1992: 193).

The end of the Cold War also contributed to facilitate a closer bilateral co-operation. Even though interdependence-related issues were not new in the bilateral relationship, in the United States, they had been overshadowed by the more dire threat of a nuclear confrontation with the Soviet Union. By the end of the Cold War, however, the United States was able to devote more attention to trans-national challenges. Since trans-border issues with Mexico were the outcome of interdependence, their very nature created the need to confront them in a more collaborative way (Cope 1997: 242–3). In the long term, they were deemed to represent the main threat to US society (Dziedzic 1997: 104). The end of Cold War reduced US pressure on Mexico to support US views, and for all practical purposes the country opted for "bandwagoning" with the United States (Dominguez and Fernandez 2001: 22). That is, Mexico assumed a "pragmatic" approach regarding its neighbor to the north in order to reduce its vulnerability in the context of an asymmetric relationship (Escude 2009: 7).

Even though NAFTA was promoted as nothing more than a trade agreement during the negotiation process, it had important security implications for North America as a whole:

> As the tapestry of the three societies [Canada, the United States and Mexico] becomes more intricately interwoven, however, any fraying at the edges of one social order would have unavoidable consequences for the others. In this way, NAFTA could unintentionally create the necessity for future security cooperation.
>
> (Dziedzic 1995: 2)

That is, NAFTA was far from being purely a trade agreement that would not have any significant political or security implications; to the extent that the three societies have been more tightly bound together, each has acquired a vested interest in the stability of the others. This basically meant an interest in Mexico's stability, due to the potential for social dislocations within the country resulting from the new economic model.

There is agreement regarding the point that NAFTA increased US economic stakes in Mexico, and in so doing heightened the urgency of defending US interests in the case of potential instability in Mexico. Following this rationale, US-Mexican economic integration must be followed by military integration, which, in turn, has to be justified in terms of the need to address crime and drug trafficking in Mexico. According to a perspective, "it is precisely in these circumstances that Mexican national security has transformed itself into regional security, largely in response to trans-national capital and US strategic interests"; Mexican security, therefore, became susceptible to being defined by the United States (Rochlin 1997: 180–4).

If it is true that in principle NAFTA was only a trade pact, it has also entailed political consequences such as the imperative of a closer security co-operation between the two countries. In the opinion of a former US ambassador to Mexico, for instance, "from a foreign policy perspective, an FTA [free trade agreement] would institutionalize acceptance of a North American orientation to Mexico's foreign policy" (quoted by Perez 1995: 130). A similar view establishes that "for a document that does not explicitly mention security matters, NAFTA is nevertheless replete with implications for regional security cooperation" (Dziedzic 1995: 2). These opinions support the idea that the higher the economic stakes in the bilateral relationship, the higher the pressure to maintain Mexico's stability, as noted earlier.

The specific expression of this atmosphere of "co-operation" has been Mexico's apparent willingness to increase military collaboration with its neighbor to the north. Although military contacts between the United States and Mexico had not been extensive – due to a history of US interventionism – they have nonetheless gradually increased, and one of the prime areas for bilateral co-operation has been the so-called "war on drugs".

This argument, nevertheless, contrasts sharply with others for which NAFTA is actually an opportunity to manage trans-national threats more than a mere *façade* to control social unrest in Mexico (Sweeney 1996: 5). Rochlin's perspective is also at odds with the view expressed by Schulz earlier, for whom trans-border security concerns are serious enough to be relevant by themselves, independently of NAFTA. If it is true that the agreement increased US concerns about the need to avoid trans-border risks from Mexico, the irony is that these challenges have been in part the side-effects of the US-supported neo-liberal reform in Mexico.

In theory, NAFTA has made it difficult for Mexico to conceive its national security without taking into account the external environment, a situation that would be further emphasized by the terrorist attacks in the United States, as security surpassed the economy at the top of the bilateral agenda. In terms of trans-border challenges, nevertheless, even before the 9/11 attacks, it had been suggested that "Mexico [had to] be understood by the US military establishment as an area that may pose unique asymmetric threats to [US] national security in the not so distant future" (Pappas 1998: 24). It was noted, for instance, that the US border with Mexico should be seen as an "appealing avenue" not only for illicit flows, but also for the possible infiltration of "foreign terrorists bent on delivering weapons of mass destruction" (Pappas 1998: 19).

This line of argument has often been used as a disguise to justify a hardline against undocumented immigration, and it has provided the rationale behind proposals pointing out that the best way to secure the US Southwest border is through its "formal militarization" (Ramirez 1999: 28). Fighting terrorism at the border, in fact, is one of the priorities established by the US Border Patrol strategy (CBP 2020: 4), even though this can also be seen as a convenient pretext for securing support and resources to basically continue dealing with undocumented immigration.

According to the aforementioned discussion, if it is true that the United States has been Mexico's main external concern, issues affecting the bilateral relationship and a closer economic integration with its neighbor to the north have made Mexico more vulnerable to international developments, especially after NAFTA entered into force. Furthermore, after 9/11, Mexico also became exposed to international terrorism not because the country is a target of these organizations per se, but because of its adjacency to the United States and the intensity of their relationship, and therefore for the possibility for terrorists to attack US interests in Mexican territory, such as critical infrastructure at the common border or US tourists in Mexico. This is just one of the reasons why the country is obliged to change its historically inward-looking "national security" outlook.

Bibliography

Aguayo, S. (1993). "The Uses, Misuses, and Challenges of Mexican National Security: 1946–1990". In B. M. Bagley and S. Aguayo (Eds.), *Mexico. In Search of Security* (p. 98), North-South Center, University of Miami. New Brunswick, NJ: Transaction Publishers by the University of Miami.

Aguilar-Camin, H., and Meyer, L. (1993). *In the Shadow of the Mexican Revolution. Contemporary Mexican History, 1910–1989.* Institute of Latin American Studies (ILAS), University of Texas, Austin. Austin: University of Texas Press.

Bailey, J., and Shelton-Colby, S. (October 9, 1992). *U.S. and Mexican National Interests and Strategic Options in the Post-Cold War Era.* Background Paper prepared for Working Meeting at Tepoztlan, Morelos. Center for Latin American Studies. Georgetown University.

Camara de Diputados del H. Congreso de la Union. (December 20, 2019a). *Constitucion Politica de los Estados Unidos Mexicanos.* Constitucion publicada en el Diario Oficial de la Federacion el 5 de febrero de 1917. Retrieved from: http://www.diputados.gob.mx/LeyesBiblio/pdf/1_201219.pdf

Camara de Diputados del H. Congreso de la Union. (November 8, 2019b). *Ley de Seguridad Nacional.* Nueva Ley publicada en el Diario Oficial de la Federacion el 31 de enero de 2005. Retrieved from: http://www.diputados.gob.mx/LeyesBiblio/pdf/LSegNac_081119.pdf

Chase, R. S., Hill, E. B., and Kennedy, P. (January/February, 1996). "Pivotal States and U.S. Strategy". *Foreign Affairs.* Vol. 75, No. 1, 37.

Cope, J. A. (1997). "En Busca de la Convergencia: Las Relaciones Militares entre Mexico y Estados Unidos". In S. Aguayo and B. M. Bailey (Eds.), *Las Seguridades de México y Estados Unidos en un Momento de Transición* (pp. 242–243). Mexico: Siglo XXI Editores.

Cornelius, W. A. (1996). *Mexican Politics in Transition. The Breakdown of a One-Party-Dominant Regime.* Monograph series Num. 41. Center for U.S.-Mexican Studies. San Diego: University of California.

Dominguez, J. I., and Fernandez de Castro, R. (2001). *The United States and Mexico. Between Partnership and Conflict.* Contemporary Inter-American Relations. New York, NY: Routledge.

Dziedzic, M. J. (1985). "Mexico". In D. J. Murray and P. R. Viotti (Eds.), *The Defense Policies of Nations. A Comparative Study* (2nd Ed., pp. 111, 114). Baltimore, MD: The Johns Hopkins University Press.

Dziedzic, M. J. (1989). "Mexico: Converging Challenges". *Adelphy Papers.* No. 242. London: Brassey's for The International Institute for Strategic Studies (IISS).

Dziedzic, M. J. (1997). "Mexico en la Gran Estrategia de Estados Unidos: Eje Geoestrategico para la Seguridad y la Prosperidad". In S. Aguayo and B. M. Bailey (Eds.), *Las Seguridades de Mexico y Estados Unidos en un momento de transicion* (p. 104). México: Siglo XXI Editores.

Dziedzic, M. J. (January, 1995). "NAFTA and North American Security". *Strategic Forum*, No. 18.

The Editors of Encyclopaedia Britannica. (September 20, 2018). "Institutional Revolutionary Party". *Encyclopaedia Britannica.* Retrieved from: https://www.britannica.com/topic/Institutional-Revolutionary-Party

Escude, C. (September, 2009). "Realismo Periferico. Una Filosofía de Politica Exterior para Estados Debiles". Serie *Documentos de Trabajo.* No. 406. Buenos Aires, Argentina: Universidad del CEMA.

Garmone, J. (January 29, 2019). *DOD Officials Testify on Military Support to Southwest Border.* U.S. Department of Defense. Retrieved from: https://www.defense.gov/Explore/News/Article/Article/1743120/dod-officials-testify-on-military-support-to-southwest-border/

Gonzalez, G. (1989). "Tradiciones y Premisas de la Politica Exterior de Mexico". In R. Green and P. H. Smith (Eds.), *La Política y la Agenda Mexico-Estados Unidos* (p. 36). Trabajos Preparados para la Comision sobre el Futuro de las Relaciones Mexico-Estados Unidos. Mexico: Fondo de Cultura Economica.

Grayson, G. W. (1999). *Mexico's Armed Forces. A Factbook*. A Military Studies Report of the CSIS Americas Program. Mexico Project. Washington, DC: Center for Strategic and International Studies.

Herrera-Lasso, L., and Gonzalez, G. (1990). "Balance y Perspectivas en el Uso del Concepto de la Seguridad Nacional en el Caso de Mexico". En S. Aguayo y b. M. Bagley. (Eds.). (1990). *En Busca de la Seguridad Perdida. Aproximaciones a la Seguridad Nacional Mexicana* (p. 391). Mexico: Siglo XXI Editores.

Interviews carried out on February 25, 2020 in Mexico City with high-ranking officials from Centro de Estudios Superiores Navales (CESNAV) and Colegio de Defensa Nacional (CODENAL).

Leal-Buitrago, F. (June 15, 2003). "La Doctrina de Seguridad Nacional: Materializacion de la Guerra Fria en America del Sur". *Revista de Estudios Sociales*. Guerra II. Retrieved from: https://revistas.uniandes.edu.co/doi/pdf/10.7440/res15.2003.05

Mares, D. R. (1996). "Intereses Estrategicos en la Relacion Mexico-Estados Unidos". In S. Aguayo and B. M. Bailey (Eds.), *Las Seguridades de Mexico y Estados Unidos en un Momento de Transicion* (p. 41). Mexico: Siglo XXI Editores.

Merrill, T. L., and Miro, R. (Eds.). (1997). *Mexico. A Country Study*. Federal Research Division. Washington, DC: Library of Congress.

Navarro, A. W. (2010). *Political Intelligence and the Creation of Modern Mexico, 1938–1954*. University Park: Penn State University Press.

Pappas, G. A. (April, 1998). *Our Own Backyard: Mexico and US National Security*. SSC Fellow, Strategic Research Project. USAWAC Class of 1998. Carlisle Barracks, PA: US Army War College.

Pastor, R. A. (July, 1992). *The Carter Administration and Latin America: A Test of Principle*, The Carter Center. Retrieved from://www.cartercenter.org/documents/1243.pdf

Paz, M. E. (1997). *Strategy, Security, and Spies. Mexico and the US as Allies in World War II*. University Park: The Pennsylvania State University Press.

Pellicer, O. (1983). "National Security in Mexico: Traditional Notions and New Preoccupations". In C. W. Reynolds and C. Tello (Eds.), *U.S.-Mexico Relations* (p. 188). Stanford, CA: Stanford University Press.

Perez, A. I. (1995). "Free Trade with Mexico and US National Security". In D. E. Schultz and E. J. Williams (Eds.), *Mexico Faces the 21st Century* (p. 130). Westport, CT: Praeger Publishers.

Piñeyro, J. L. (September, 1995). "La Politica de Defensa de Mexico frente al TLC: Algunas Reflexiones". *El Cotidiano*. No. 71.

Purcell, S. K. (February, 1993). "Mexico's New Economic Vitality". *Current History*. Vol. 91, 54.

Ramirez, J. E. (April, 1999). *The New Front Line: Militarization of the US-Mexico Border*. Strategic Research Project. USAWAC Class of 1999. Carlisle Barracks, PA: US Army War College.

Rochlin, J. F. (1997). *Redefining Mexican 'Security': Society, State & Region under NAFTA*. Boulder, CO: Lynne Rienner Publishers.

Ronfeldt, D. (1984). "The Modern Mexican Military: An Overview". In D. Ronfeldt (Ed.), *The Modern Mexican Military: A Reassessment* (p. 11). Monograph Series 15. La Jolla, CA: Center for U.S.- Mexican Studies; San Diego: University of California.

Sanchez David, R., and Rodriguez Morales, F. A. (Second Semester, 2006). "Seguridad Nacional: El Realismo y sus Contradictores". *Desafíos*. No. 15. Retrieved from: https://media.proquest.com/media/hms/PFT/1/2odoC?_s=AHyQfBcGoE3f%2FPS6CvjqoREXUL0%3D

Schulz, D. E. (1999). "The United States and Latin America: A Strategic Perspective". In M. G. Manwaring (Ed.), *Security and Civil-Military Relations in the New World Disorder: The Use of Armed Forces in the Americas* (p. 10). An Anthology from a Symposium Cosponsored by the Chief of Staff, United States Army. Kingsville, TX: The George Bush School of Government and Public Service, and the US Army War College.

Secretaria de la Defensa Nacional (SEDENA)/Secretaria de Marina-Armada de Mexico (SEMAR). (February 27, 2018). *Glosario de Terminos Unificados de Seguridad Nacional*. Colegio de Defensa Nacional (CODENAL)/Centro de Estudios Superiores Navales (CESNAV). Mimeograph.

Sweeney, J. (March 6, 1996). "Fulfilling the Promise of NAFTA: A New Strategy for U.S.-Mexican Relations". *Backgrounder*. The Heritage Foundation, No. 1070.

United Nations. (January 31, 2020). *Contributors to UN Peacekeeping Operations by Country and Post: Police, UN Military Experts on Mission, Staff Officers and Troops*. Merged Gender Report. Retrieved from: https://peacekeeping.un.org/sites/default/files/1_summary_of_contributions_20.pdf

U.S. Customs and Border Protection (CBP). (2020). *2020 US Border Patrol Strategy*. Department of Homeland Security (DHS). Retrieved from: https://www.cbp.gov/sites/default/files/assets/documents/2019-Sep/2020-USBP-Strategy.pdf

Weintraub, S., and M. D. Baer, M. D. (Spring, 1992). "The Interplay between Economic and Political Opening: The Sequence in Mexico". *The Washington Quarterly*. Vol. 15, No. 2, 193.

Whitehead, L. (1991). "Mexico and the 'Hegemony' of the United States: Past, Present, and Future". In R. Roett (Ed.), *Mexico's External Relations in the 1990s* (p. 245). Boulder, CO: Lynne Rienner Publishers, Inc.

The White House. (November 21, 1978). "Presidential Review Memorandum NSC-41: Review of U.S. Policies toward Mexico". National Security Council. *Presidential Directives on National Security from Truman to Clinton, National Security Archive*. Washington, DC: The George Washington University.

World Bank Data. (2019). *Military Expenditure (% of GDP)*. Washington, DC: The World Bank. Retrieved from: https://data.worldbank.org/indicator/ms.mil.xpnd.gd.zs

3 Conceptualization

Who Defines National Security?

3.1 National Development Plans

This chapter explains how, based on a strong presidentialism that has not subsided with democratic change, national security in Mexico has traditionally been defined by the President according to the defense of the sovereignty and economic development objectives established in the Constitution, and reflected in the six-year-term development plans of each administration. It addresses the LSN as the main official document that presumably articulates national security, and underlines the misleading name of the law because, far from regulating a system, it is rather oriented to provide a legal framework for the activities of the civilian intelligence agency. It also discusses one of the sources of confusion in Mexico about national security, which is the fact that misunderstanding is built into the legislation as the concept of national security comprises internal security, in the process mixing the instruments at the disposal of the state to address different challenges.

Due to the nature of the Mexican political system, which allowed the civilian leadership to deliberately keep away the armed forces from politics, the definition of national security has been the responsibility of the politicians, specifically of the President, both during the tenures of PRI governments and its successors. Mexico has had a solid presidential tradition, and democratic change has not had an impact on the security sector, as decisions continue to be made at the highest echelons of the civilian leadership. This did not mean that the military has had no voice. It rather meant that while the armed forces have had autonomy to make decisions on budgetary and professional matters, national security policy has been kept as a purview of civilian officials.

Table 3.1 National Development Plans, from Lopez-Portillo to Lopez Obrador

President	*Jose Lopez-Portillo (PRI)*	*Miguel de la Madrid (PRI)*	*Carlos Salinas (PRI)*	*Ernesto Zedillo (PRI)*
PND	*1980–1982*	*1983–1988*	*1989–1994*	*1995–2000*
Definition	Not provided	Integral development of the nation, as an essential tool to keep liberty, peace and social justice	Not provided	Not provided
Objectives	Independence	Sovereignty; democratic regime	Sovereignty; economic development; rights of Mexicans abroad; international cooperation	Sovereignty through: improving national security; active foreign policy; shared responsibility regarding global issues such as drug trafficking
Instruments	Internal policy, foreign policy, national security, administration of justice	Foreign policy; armed forces	Foreign policy; armed forces	Foreign policy; armed forces
Actions	Economic development	Promote peace and justice abroad; integral development domestically	Economic diversification; international cooperation; supporting East-West distention; fair trade; combatting drug trafficking	Territorial integrity; rule of law; updating the armed forces planning; coordination to combat drugs; intelligence legal framework
Challenges	Exhaustion of previous economic model	Domestic crisis, uncertain international context	Transformation of the international context	Interference in Mexican politics

Vicente Fox (PAN)	*Felipe Calderon (PAN)*	*Enrique Peña-Nieto (PRI)*	*Andres Manuel Lopez-Obrador (MORENA)*
2001–2006	*2007–2012*	*2013–2018*	*2019–2024*
Protection and preservation of the collective interest, preventing or minimizing, when possible, any risk or threat to the physical integrity of the population and institutions	Not provided	Essential function of the state, fundamental right of citizens	Indispensable condition to guarantee national sovereignty and integrity, free of threats to the state, in order to build a fruitful and lasting peace
Independence and sovereignty; new strategic framework for national security; democratic governability	Territorial integrity; sovereignty	Population, sovereignty, independence, territorial integrity, constitutional order, democratic institutions, unity, defense against external actors, development	To change "war measures" for an integral peace and security policy to combat the root causes of criminality and loss of security
Armed forces;	Armed forces; international cooperation;	National Security System; Culture of National Security; Strengthening the armed forces; National Intelligence System	Amnesty; social mobility; end prohibition; transitional justice; National Intelligence System; Culture of National Security; National Guard
Protect the territory; modernize the armed forces; Democratic control of the intelligence apparatus	Promote ordered migration flows; border security	Design of public policies based on a multidimensional security perspective	Anti-corruption; reforming anti-drug operations; prison reform; National Guard; improve coordination
No external threats, but need to respond to global issues	Illegal flow of drugs, people and arms	Poverty, lack of education, health, environment, cyberthreats	Dealing with violence through coercive means

Article 89, Section VI of the Constitution, establishes as one of the President's responsibilities to preserve national security, employing the armed forces for the "internal security and external defense of the federation" (Camara de Diputados 2019: 88a). Formally, the notion of national security has been reflected in the six-year-term National Development Plans (PND). Beyond the national security objectives set for in the Constitution, which are the "permanent national interests", every government has adopted an additional set of goals, taking into consideration the changing domestic and, apparently, the international contexts (transitory national interests), and therefore the national security perspective has mirrored these variations over time.

The history of PNDs in Mexico dates back to the end of the 1920s with the National Economic Council Act of 1928 and the 1930 General Planning Law. It was in the 1930s when President Cardenas presented the First Sexennial Plan for the period 1934–1940, which "inaugurates in Mexico the era of economic and social policy as the maximum expression of public activity" (Martinez-Escamilla 2013: 119). This initial plan later on evolved in the subsequent PNDs. However, before references to national security found in these plans, the first mention in an official document appeared in 1973, in SEGOB regulations regarding the Federal Directorate of Security (DFS) that was responsible for incidents "related to the security of the nation" (Rodriguez-Castañeda 2013).

A review of these plans, from President Lopez-Portillo 1980–1982 "Global Development Plan", to AMLO's 2019–2024 PND, shows that not all documents have provided a specific definition of national security. Those which define it contain elements such as "integral development", "protection and preservation of the collective interest", "essential function of the state and fundamental right of citizens", and "indispensable condition". As a more developed definition, Peña-Nieto's plan advocated a broader concept of security to incorporate poverty, education, diseases, environmental, economic, social, cultural, and technology issues, that is, to conceive national security from a multidimensional perspective (DOF 2013: 14).

The majority of the plans, nevertheless, include independence and defense of sovereignty as fundamental objectives, as well as the importance of upholding democracy. For instance, Lopez-Portillo's plan did not define the concept of national security, but it is implicit in one of the program's four fundamental objectives, which is to "reaffirm and strengthen the independence of Mexico as a democratic, fair and economic-free nation, politically and culturally" (DOF 1980).

Presidents Zedillo and Peña Nieto's objectives incorporate the impact of global issues, while AMLO's goal is to address the roots of violence in the country.

AMLO's PND (2019–2024) "Change of security paradigm" section criticizes that between 2006 and 2018, the Mexican government addressed insecurity and violence through coercive actions with a "catastrophic" result. His proposal, in this context, is to change the "war measures" for a comprehensive peace and security policy to attack the root of the problem (Camara de Diputados 2019: 18d), reflected in his National Public Security Strategy that, among other objectives, proposes to establish a National Guard (Gobierno de Mexico 2019).

One of two objectives stands out from his PND, and it is "to reformulate the fight against drugs", based on the idea that the prohibitionist approach is already unsustainable and it has not translated into a reduction in consumption. It rejects the "war on drugs" and its effect of escalating a health problem into a public security one, and states that the only real possibility to address this problem is to lift prohibition and to launch reintegration and detoxification programs in a negotiated manner with both the United States and the UN (Camara de Diputados 2019: 20d).

Security is one of the most daunting challenges for the AMLO Administration, and in November 2018, he announced the National Peace and Security Plan 2018–2024 (Lopez-Obrador 2018) that proposed to deal with the roots of insecurity and the creation of the National Guard, among others. These proposals, nevertheless, are questionable not only for the possibility of a clash with the United States – as it already happened – but also because this set of initiatives do not seem to address the problem in the short term. These measures are considered "too simplistic" (Felbab-Brown 2019: 6), even though AMLO is correct in his central assumption that the primary security objective in the country is to reduce violence. However, "it is naïve in its expectation that reducing violence can be accomplished without focusing on drug trafficking and, more importantly, by not focusing on drug trafficking groups" (Felbab-Brown 2019: 34), as they are precisely the main sponsors of violence in the country.

Moreover, even though AMLO had promised during his campaign to return the military to its barracks (Arteta 2018), he proposed the creation of a National Guard made up from elements from the former Federal Police, Military, and Navy Police units, which resulted in a controversial initiative that was considered the "institutionalization of the armed forces participation in public security", neglecting all lessons learned in the past (Mexico Center 2019). It was ironic that when the National Guard finally started operating, for instance, it was used to block Central American immigrants from entering Mexico at the southern border in the context of the 2019 caravans (Semple 2019). Moreover, creating the National Guard instead of opting for strengthening the Federal Police has been considered a "grave mistake" by throwing overboard years of a serious "institution building" process (Valdes 2018).

In terms of instruments, most of the PNDs identify foreign policy and the armed forces as fundamental tools. Since President Zedillo's plan, attention has also gradually been accorded to intelligence. It was actually the first occasion that intelligence is referred to in a PND, in relation to the need to update its legal framework and take advantage of the exchange of information with international partners to confront transnational threats (DOF 1995: 12).

It is interesting to note that in most plans, the armed forces are clearly identified as a national security instrument (i.e. against external threats), even though their main role has been its participation in public security activities. Similarly, the increasing recognition of intelligence as a national security asset has not been reflected in a far-reaching reform in this area. This, notwithstanding the fact that President Fox's PND included a critique in the sense that in the past, intelligence agencies were used "to justify illegitimate acts of authority" whose purpose was the continuity of the regime in a context in which political opposition represented a threat to the interests of the group in power. This situation led to a discredit of these institutions and an abandonment of fundamental national security tasks (DOF 2001: 103). A legal framework and a systematized risk agenda were thus required.

As a strategy, President Fox's PND made reference to the need of modernizing the armed forces in accordance with national security priorities (DOF 2001: 106), developing new definitions of national interest and security that converge on democratic governance – conceiving national security from a broader perspective – subjecting intelligence to government controls, establishing a national security doctrine that provided for effective protection against risks and threats, and defining a national security risk agenda (DOF 2001: 108–9).

Even though his administration represented an initial effort to transform national security decision-making in Mexico, inter-bureaucratic rivalries tilted the scale at the end toward the continuation of the authoritarian model; as the first president of the alternance and notwithstanding his reformist drive, for instance, Fox missed the opportunity to separate Mexico's civilian intelligence agency, CISEN from

SEGOB, to fuse SEDENA and SEMAR into a consolidated Secretary of Defense, maintaining instead the security structures and the non-democratic *status quo* (Benitez 2008: 185–6). There was no transformation of the national security concept, and the change of security structures in the United States after 9/11 did not lead to the adaptation of counterparts in Mexico; on the contrary, it led to disagreement on the creation of the US Northern Command (NORTHCOM) by Mexico being included in its area of responsibility (Benitez 2008: 189–93), thus ignoring the fact that this was essentially an internal US bureaucratic reorganization.

In President Calderon's PND (2007–2011), defense of sovereignty and the integrity of the territory required strengthening the capabilities of the armed forces and improving border security, which demanded order and legality in migratory and commercial flows (DOF 2007: 23–4). Border security, in turn, required international cooperation as a fundamental instrument to deal with organized crime in relation to weapons, people, and drugs, and the exchange of information to control traffic and consumption of narcotics (DOF 2007: 25–6), and this orientation in part explains the logic behind the Merida Initiative.

An interesting refinement in terms of instruments and strategies was Peña-Nieto's plan to consolidate a National Security System as the guiding principle of actions to preserve the integrity, stability, and permanence of the Mexican state (DOF 2013: 15), fostering a "Culture of National Security" and strengthening civil intelligence, as well as providing legal support for the actions of the armed forces (DOF 2013: 62–3). Peña-Nieto came to power, nevertheless, with the ultimate objective of achieving the structural reforms the country required under his "Pact for Mexico", and in this context, security policy was put for all practical purposes in the backburner, becoming incomplete and ill-defined.

The Merida Initiative was put on hold by channeling all collaboration with the United States through SEGOB; the promised more efficient internal coordination was not achieved; and security policy repeated the Calderon-era measures, such as resorting once again to the armed forces to support the Federal Police, and to high-value targeting, as a response to drug-related violence (Felbab-Brown 2014: iii–iv).

There is a wide variety of actions proposed in the PNDs and these, like the objectives, have changed over time. They have included, from promoting economic development as a fundamental national interest in times of economic crises such as in President de la Madrid's plan (DOF 1983), to the adaptation of Mexico's foreign policy to the post-Cold War context under Salinas, and the adoption of a multidimensional national security approach to deal with the issues brought about by globalization proposed by Fox and Peña-Nieto.

It is revealing that several of the challenges identified in these plans are related to external factors; yet, the country's national security structure has not been reformed to respond to the government's own diagnostic of the international environment, given its continued focus on internal challenges. If it is true that the government has continually adapted to respond to drug trafficking, there is a gap between the diagnosis on paper and the actions on the ground.

For instance, first, even though the Lopez-Portillo PND did not make any reference to the external environment, paradoxically, his administration would become very active in supporting Central American centrist and leftist political forces in the region, taking advantage of the so-called "oil-boom".

Second, President Salinas PND (1989–1994) pointed out that foreign policy was a means of protecting Mexico's national interests, which were to promote sovereignty, economic development, the rights of Mexicans abroad, international cooperation, and the image of Mexico in the world (DOF 1989: 44–6). It is argued, nevertheless, that his administration in fact created a situation of "increasing insecurity", where the national goals of democracy, economic growth, social justice, and sovereignty were not completely achieved (Piñeyro 1994: 759). Growing US pressures on Mexico regarding drug trafficking actually diminished its autonomy, in a context of political pragmatism in which bilateral cooperation became a priority at all costs in order to promote economic integration as a "historic opportunity" (Piñeyro 1994: 760–9).

Third, a similar situation occurred with President Zedillo's PND (1995–2000), which stated that nationalism was the basis of sovereignty, which had to be guaranteed in a context in which Mexico had a more relevant place in the world stage not only in its contiguous area, but in the Ibero-American region (DOF 1995: 9). There was a continuity, nevertheless, from Zedillo to Salinas because of an ongoing vulnerability created by economic policy, in particular a growing dependence on the United States (Piñeyro 2001: 940).

During Zedillo's term, there was an increasing institutionalization of the relationship with the United States as a result of NAFTA. After taking office in December 1994, Zedillo declared drug trafficking as "Mexico's number one security threat" (GAO 1996: 18), and increased cooperation with the United States. Both governments signed the *Declaration of the United States-Mexico Alliance Against Drugs*, which established a High-Level Contact Group (HLCG) to provide with Cabinet-level coordination twice a year through a variety of working groups, and jointly developed the *United States/Mexico Binational Drug Strategy* announced in February 1998 (The White House 1998: 2). In this context, "there is an almost total acceptance of the US strategy that tends to infringe in [Mexican] national sovereignty even more" (Piñeyro 2001: 955). Moreover, President's Zedillo response to continuing police corruption in Mexico, as before, was to turn once again to the military to combat drug trafficking and therefore to its increasing exposure to corruption.

An analysis of the PNDs shows that although there has been a constant concern for the defense of sovereignty, independence, and territorial integrity, there has actually been a gap between the discourse that alludes to external issues, and the adequacy of institutions and policies to deal with a changing international context, since national security concerns have been dominated by domestic issues, in particular drug trafficking. Comparing the plans of Fox and Peña-Nieto to what existed before, however, it is possible to observe a qualitative change, more systematization, and sophistication, but no substantive modification regarding an outward-looking orientation, nor political will or, for that matter, capacity, to design a security policy oriented to the exterior.

Interest in reforming national security – and dealing with the exterior by definition – is present in the political discourse, such as in AMLO's plan to create a National Intelligence System mentioned earlier, but there is not any single policy implemented toward that end, for instance, or the creation of a permanent National Security Council staff to advise the President and to reflect the supposedly greater attention to world affairs.

3.2 2005 National Security Law

The LSN is the main official document in Mexico that provides a definition of national security. Nevertheless, the law reflects the existing confusion about this subject in the country because, far for establishing the basis for a National Security System, the law actually focuses on regulating the activities of the Mexican intelligence agency, CISEN, making evident a series of misconceptions that is important to correct through an entirely new legislation, one law to finally create a National Security System, and another one to organize and supervise the intelligence community.

An early antecedent of Mexican intelligence can be traced back to the creation of the First Section at SEGOB in 1918 under President Venustiano Carranza (CISEN 2014). In the 1920s, in the aftermath of the Mexican Revolution, a group of Army officers were given the task of collecting information to protect the President from the political conspiracies and internal threats that had characterized competition among *caudillos* during the revolution. In particular, in 1929, the "Confidential Department" was established within SEGOB to collect political information, and this institution basically became "Mexico's secret police". Ten years later, President Cardenas changed the name to Office of Political Information (OPI), emphasizing political and social issues (Medina 2015: 69).

In 1942, in the context of WWII, OPI became the "Social and Political Investigations Department" to keep a track of political and social movements, the activities of foreigners in Mexico, and of any subversive activities. A relevant change occurred in the context of the Cold War, when President Miguel Aleman (1946–1952) created in 1947 the DFS, based on previous secret police forces and with assistance from the US Federal Bureau of Investigation (FBI) and the Central Intelligence Agency (CIA) (Medina 2015: 70). This new organization focused almost exclusively on domestic matters, political espionage, counterinsurgency, law enforcement, and anti-communist operations. As the military threatened the stability and consolidation of the civilian government in the 1940s and 1950s, a key factor in getting them away from the Presidency was to give them control of security and intelligence agencies. In this context, the removal of the armed forces from participation in politics and its subordination to the civilian leadership, as already mentioned, was key to Mexico's stability and critical to the PRI's rule (Navarro 2010).

By the mid-1970s, the DFS was infiltrated by Mexican drug cartels and criminal organizations. Its agents were involved in drug trafficking, abuse of authority, illegal activities, political espionage, and violations of human rights. Its participation in the murder of a high-profile journalist in 1984 (Manuel Buendia) and, in February 1985, in the assassination of Drug Enforcement Administration (DEA) Special Agent in Mexico, Enrique Camarena-Salazar, apparently carried out by elements of the DFS in collusion with drug traffickers (quoted by Reuter and Ronfeldt 1992: 105), was the beginning of the end for the organization.

This incident precipitated one of the most difficult periods in US-Mexican relations and because of the scandal and US pressure, President de la Madrid disbanded the DFS in 1985 (Medina 2015: 70).

Most DFS agents were fired and a decision was made to incorporate the few reliable officers into a newly created institution, the Directorate of Investigation and National Security (DISEN). Change was real because the new agency would only focus on intelligence, leaving operations altogether, and its agenda would not cover drug trafficking, a responsibility that would go to the General Attorney's Office (PGR) (Leroy 2004: 110). Under President Salinas, DISEN became CISEN in February 1989, and the agency started a development process by incorporating new technology and establishing its first contacts with foreign intelligence services (Herrera-Lasso 2010: 202).

Political alternation in Mexico, with the triumph of Fox in the presidential election in 2000, represented the first time an opposition candidate won the Presidency after 71 years of continued PRI domination. As other opposition politicians ever suspicious of the intelligence service being used by the government for political purposes, during his campaign, and after assuming the Presidency, Fox and his team led a public debate about the role, scope, and potential limits of Mexican intelligence (Medina 2015: 71). The perception was that CISEN had been created by the PRI to serve its interests and that it had been used to suppress political opposition. Getting rid of CISEN was the solution (Herrera-Lasso 2010: 212). Fox was advised about the convenience of taking advantage of the "democratic bonus" provided by his electoral victory to reform Mexican institutions, and in this context during his inauguration, he ordered an assessment of the CISEN to be presented within three months (Herrera-Lasso 2010: 202).

By the end of the review process, the outcome disappointed some in the Fox Administration. It turned out that CISEN was a solid and responsible institution, it had achieved a reasonable degree of professionalization by establishing, since 1994, a clear career path based on merit, as well as an efficient recruitment process based on testing and screening, leaving behind personal recommendations to become members of the service, and there was no evidence that the institution had been infiltrated by drug trafficking (Herrera-Lasso 2010: 202). On the downside, its main challenge was the lack of a legal framework for its activities, since CISEN had been operating under SEGOB internal regulations and under supervision of its own Comptroller's Office (Herrera-Lasso 2010: 215).

Therefore, a consensus began to build up within the Mexican Congress about the need to provide a legal basis. After winning the Presidency, the government of the alternation announced in June 2002 that the files kept in CISEN archives would be made available to the public. With this access, an interesting account documented the history of the "dirty war" in Mexico and how the DFS was used to suppress political dissidence in the country, and also how its leadership exaggerated the threat posed by guerrilla movements and the opposition to advance their political careers. Its conclusion was also the need of a legal framework for the service, in order to prevent abuse of power (see Aguayo 2001).

In this context, in 2005, the National Security Law was approved by the Congress, based on a 1994 legislative project prepared by CISEN itself that was never submitted by the Executive. The law, however, reflected an unmistakable confusion about what national security is all about. Congress passed a piece of legislation titled "National Security Law", which, far from organizing and providing for a National Security System, was basically a law to regulate CISEN's activities, in particular the requirement for a judicial order before intercepting electronic communications. It established a National Security Council to replace the National Security Cabinet, as well as a Bicameral Commission in Congress to supervise intelligence activities (Camara de Diputados 2019c).

This legislation presented several problems. First, one of its articles defined both national security, as mentioned earlier, and threats to national security. As far as the latter is concerned, establishing threats in the law does not make sense, given the fact that threats are dynamic, always evolving. It makes more sense to describe the permanent national interests and the means to achieve them in the face of potential challenges. Second, if it is true that the law provided for the establishment of a National Security Council, control judges to approve communications interventions and the Bicameral Commission, the Council was only a deliberative body, and the Commission was loosely organized without any effective mechanism to supervise the CISEN, nor any vetting process to provide for a secure clearance system to regulate access to information (Vignettes 2019: 316). Therefore, the task of approving a real National Security Law in Mexico is still pending, and it is actually a step that should be a consequence of a redefinition of national security in the country.

Both the fact that CISEN had been under SEGOB and the law regulating its activities being called "National Security Law" show a serious lack of understanding of national security, as well as a considerable gap separating official rhetoric and reality.

3.3 First Complication: The Legal Framework

One of the reasons why there is confusion in Mexico among the concepts of national, internal, and public security is precisely because this misunderstanding is built into the legislation, especially in regard to internal security, which is considered to be an integral part of national security. While it is true that internal security challenges can escalate to national security issues, and the fact that internal security challenges in Mexico are very serious, the same reason requires conceptual clarity in order to apply the terms correctly.

For instance, Article 89 of the Constitution, on the powers and obligations of the President, Section VI, states "to preserve national security, in the terms of the respective law, and to have a permanent armed force, that is, the Army, the Navy and the Air Force, for the internal security and external defense of the Federation" (Camara de Diputados 2019: 88a). That is, national security includes interior security and therefore the use of military force for domestic purposes is contemplated. This confusion passes on from the Constitution to the laws and sectorial programs. The LSN, in its Article 3, states that "national security means actions aimed immediately and directly to maintain the integrity, stability and permanence of the Mexican State, which contribute to:... (III) The maintenance of the constitutional order and the strengthening of democratic government institutions" (Camara de Diputados 2019: 2c). As for national security programs, the one of 2009–2012 replicates the provisions of the LSN (DOF 2009), and that of 2014–2018 does exactly the same (Mexico 2014: 31).

This conceptualization has created in Mexico a situation where an instrument par excellence to guarantee national security – such as the armed forces – has been used for decades without proper constitutional authorization, to contribute to internal order in the face of the challenge posed by drug-related violence, and in response to police corruption and lack of adequate equipment. While in developed countries this has also happened because of the need to seek new missions for the armed forces, particularly in relation to non-traditional threats after the Cold War, in the case of Mexico, the country has been forced to confront drug trafficking also to keep at bay the United States (Dominguez and Fernandez 2001: 43).

The use of the military, however, has not been suitable for facing Mexico's internal challenges, not only for exposing the armed forces to corruption, but also for the violation of human rights. For instance, violation of human rights quintupled during the so-called "Calderon war" (Speck 2019: 72). Given this situation, President Peña-Nieto sent in December 2017 an initiative to Congress to provide for a legal framework for the participation of the armed forces in public security tasks, which was approved that same year, only to be subsequently suspended by a ruling of the Supreme Court because of a constitutional dispute (Hernandez 2018), by basically expanding the armed forces' jurisdiction over the civilian population. According to a specialist, the law represented "the normative consecration of the discretionary and systematic use of the armed forces, apart from the declaration of the state of exception embodied in Article 29 of the Constitution" (Moloeznik 2019: 148), which is recommended by the International Committee of the Red Cross only under extraordinary circumstances. This generates de facto states of exception, where the armed forces intervene. On May 11, 2020, nevertheless, the AMLO government published the decree authorizing the armed forces to carry out public security activities, thus formalizing the militarization of security in the country (DOF 2020).

While the armed forces support internal and public security in other parts of the world, this cannot be normal, as this implies risks, for instance, the level of subordination of the military to civilians, the rule of law and the rights of citizens, and the very reduction of the role of the armed forces when employed in police duties (GTSR 2013: 3). It means degrading the armed forces and transforming them into mere subsidiary guards of the security forces. Most importantly, the participation of the armed forces has not changed the situation and has not made a difference. Employing the military could generate more risks in Mexico if it erodes the civilian control of the military creating political instability, which would be even more serious than drug trafficking itself for the United States, which happens to be the main instigator of their participation in public security activities. Under AMLO, an increasing number of non-military tasks assigned to the armed forces (i.e. public works) are considered to go against carefully designed civilian control of the military in Mexico (Tirado 2020).

An alternative to the military's participation in public security consists in promoting a culture of prevention and to think of a new model through the creation of vetted, small police units that begin to attack the most serious dynamics of crime, while the wider police force grows, is professionalized, and a culture of integrity is created before focusing on drug-related challenges. In this context, the role of the armed forces would consist in providing intelligence and logistical support for these units and then, in their role as guarantors of national security, to act to maintain land, sea, and air border security (GTSR 2013: 7).

Confusion is present not only in the distinction between national security and internal security, but between the former and public security. For example, the coercive instruments available to the President for his national security obligations under Article 89 are practically the same under other articles concerning public security. Article 21 of the Constitution indicates that public security is the responsibility of the federation, states, and municipalities, for which the federation will have the National Guard (Camara de Diputados 2019: 25a), which is in part made up of Military and Naval Police units.

According to Article 115, Section III (h), the municipalities participate in public security tasks (Camara de Diputados 2019: 25a), which is a "concurrent responsibility" that involves the three levels of government. This article, in turn, gives origin to the General Law of the National Public Security System, which, in its Article 10, Section 1, conceives the National Public Security Council as the "highest instance of coordination and definition of public policies" (Camara de Diputados 2009: 5b), that in its Article 12 establishes that it is presided by the President, with the participation of SEGOB, SEDENA, SEMAR, and the Executive Secretariat of the system, among others. According to a specialist, "it draws powerfully the attention that the military participates in the highest decision-making instance in the field of public safety" (Moloeznik 2019: 157).

Therefore, in the case of Mexico, confusion about the distinction among "national", "internal", and "public" security is by design, and this misunderstanding does not allow the government to formulate efficient public policy to confront the challenges, first of all by not having clarity about the instruments at its disposal.

Bibliography

Aguayo, S. (2001). *La Charola. Una Historia de los Servicios de Inteligencia en Mexico.* Mexico: Grijalbo.

Arteta, I. (November 21, 2018). "El Sabueso: ¿Promover Reformas Constitucionales? ¿Sacar al Ejército de las Calles? AMLO se Contradice". *Animal Politico.* Retrieved from: https://www.animalpolitico.com/elsabueso/sabueso-amlo-ejercito-contradicciones/

Benitez, R. (January/June, 2008). "La Seguridad Nacional en la Indefinida Transición: Mitos y Realidades del Sexenio de Vicente Fox". *Foro Internacional.* Vol. XLVIII, No.1–2, 185–186 and 189–193.

Bulletin of Peace Proposals. (July 1, 1986). "23. The Concept of Common Security". Vol. 17, No. 3–4. Retrieved from: https://journals.sagepub.com/doi/abs/10.1177/096701068601700325?journalCode=sdia

Calderon Hinojosa, F. (2010). *La Lucha por la Seguridad Pública.* Presidencia de la Republica. Retrieved from: http://portal.sre.gob.mx/chicago/pdf/061810SeguridadPublica.pdf

Camara de Diputados del H. Congreso de la Union. (December 20, 2019a). *Constitucion Politica de los Estados Unidos Mexicanos.* Constitucion publicada en el Diario Oficial de la Federación el 5 de febrero de 1917. Retrieved from: http://www.diputados.gob.mx/LeyesBiblio/pdf/1_201219.pdf

Camara de Diputados del H. Congreso de la Union. (May 27, 2019b). *Ley General del Sistema Nacional de Seguridad Publica.* Nueva Ley publicada en el Diario Oficial de la Federacion el 2 de enero de 2009. Retrieved from: http://www.diputados.gob.mx/LeyesBiblio/pdf/LGSNSP_270519.pdf

Camara de Diputados del H. Congreso de la Union. (November 8, 2019c). *Ley de Seguridad Nacional.* Nueva Ley publicada en el Diario Oficial de la Federacion el 31 de enero de 2005. Retrieved from: http://www.diputados.gob.mx/LeyesBiblio/pdf/LSegNac_081119.pdf

Camara de Diputados. LXIV Legislatura. (April 30, 2019d). *Plan Nacional de Desarrollo 2019–2024.* Gaceta Parlamentaria. Año XX. Numero 5266-XVIII. Retrieved from: http://gaceta.diputados.gob.mx/PDF/64/2019/abr/20190430-XVIII.pdf

CISEN. (December 18, 2014). "Reseña Histórica". SEGOB. Retrieved from: http://www.cisen.gob.mx/cisenResena.html

Diario Oficial de la Federacion (DOF). (May 11, 2020). *Acuerdo por el que se Dispone de la Fuerza Armada Permanente para Llevar a Cabo Tareas de Seguridad Publica de Manera Extraordinaria, Regulada, Fiscalizada, Subordinada y Complementaria.* Retrieved from: https://www.dof.gob.mx/nota_detalle.php?codigo=5593105&fecha=11/05/2020

Diario Oficial de la Federacion (DOF). (May 31, 1983). *Plan Nacional de Desarrollo 1983–1988.* Retrieved from: http://dof.gob.mx/nota_detalle.php?codigo=4805999&fecha=31/05/1983

Diario Oficial de la Federacion (DOF). (May 31, 1989). *Plan Nacional de Desarrollo 1989–1984.* Poder Ejecutivo Federal. Retrieved from: http://www.diputados.gob.mx/LeyesBiblio/compila/pnd/PND_1989-1994_31may89.pdf

Diario Oficial de la Federacion (DOF). (May 31, 1995). *Plan Nacional de Desarrollo 1995–2000.* Poder Ejecutivo Federal. Retrieved from: http://www.diputados.gob.mx/LeyesBiblio/compila/pnd.htm

Diario Oficial de la Federacion (DOF). (May 30, 2001). *Plan Nacional de Desarrollo 2001–2006.* Poder Ejecutivo Federal. Retrieved from: http://www.diputados.gob.mx/LeyesBiblio/compila/pnd.htm

Diario Oficial de la Federacion (DOF). (May 31, 2007). *Plan Nacional de Desarrollo 2007–2012.* Poder Ejecutivo Federal. Retrieved from: http://www.diputados.gob.mx/LeyesBiblio/compila/pnd.htm

Diario Oficial de la Federacion (DOF). (May 20, 2013). *Plan Nacional de Desarrollo 2013–2018.* Poder Ejecutivo Federal. Retrieved from: http://www.diputados.gob.mx/LeyesBiblio/compila/pnd.htm

Diario Oficial de la Federación (DOF). (August 20, 2009). *Programa para la Seguridad Nacional (2009–2012).* Retrieved from: http://www.cns.gob.mx/portalWebApp/ShowBinary?nodeId=/BEA%20Repository/578170//archivo

Diario Oficial de la Federacion (DOF). (April 17, 1980). *Version abreviada del Plan Global de Desarrollo 1980–1982.* Retrieved from: http://www.dof.gob.mx/nota_detalle.php?codigo=4851638&fecha=17/04/1980

Dominguez, J. I., and Fernandez de Castro, R. (2001). *The United States and Mexico. Between Partnership and Conflict.* Contemporary Inter-American Relations. New York, NY: Routledge.

Felbab-Brown, V. (March, 2019). *AMLO's Security Policy: Creative Ideas, Though Reality.* The Brookings Institution. Retrieved from: https://www.brookings.edu/wp-content/uploads/2019/03/FP_20190325_mexico_anti-crime.pdf

Felbab-Brown, V. (November, 2014). *Changing the Game or Dropping the Ball? Mexico's Security and Anti-Crime Strategy under President Enrique Peña Nieto.* Latin America Initiative. Foreign Policy at Brookings. Retrieved from: https://www.brookings.edu/wp-content/uploads/2016/06/mexico-security-anti-crime-nieto-v2-felbabbrown.pdf

Gobierno de Mexico. (February 1, 2019). *Estrategia Nacional de Seguridad Publica.* Retrieved from: https://www.gob.mx/cms/uploads/attachment/file/434517/Estrategia_Seguridad-ilovepdf-compressed-ilovepdf-compressed-ilovepdf-compressed__1_.pdf

Grupo de Trabajo en Seguridad Regional (GTSR)-Ecuador. (May, 2013). "Los Militares en la Seguridad Interna: Realidad y Desafíos para Ecuador". *Perspectivas.* No. 1. Retrieved from: https://library.fes.de/pdf-files/bueros/la-seguridad/10063.pdf

Hernandez, L. (November 15, 2018). "SCJN Declara Inconstitucional la Ley de Seguridad Interior". *El Economista.* Retrieved from: https://www.eleconomista.com.mx/politica/SCJN-declara-inconstitucional-la-Ley-de-Seguridad-Interior--20181115-0087.html

Herrera-Lasso, L. (2010). "Inteligencia y Seguridad Nacional: Apuntes y Reflexiones". In A. Alvarado and M. Serrano (Eds.), *Seguridad Nacional y Seguridad Interior* (pp. 202, 212 and 215). Los Grandes Problemas de Mexico, XIV. Mexico: El Colegio de Mexico.

Leroy, C. (Winter-Spring, 2004). "Mexican Intelligence at a Crossroad". *The SAIS Review of International Relations.* Vol. XXIV, No. 1, 110.

Lopez-Obrador, A. M. (2018). *Plan Nacional de Paz y Seguridad 2018–2024.* Transicion Mexico 2018–2024. Retrieved from: https://lopezobrador.org.mx/wp-content/uploads/2018/11/Plan-Nacional-de-Paz-y-Seguridad_.pdf

Martinez-Escamilla, R. (2013). "El Plan Sexenal de Gobierno 1934–40 como Modelo de Desarrollo". *Problemas del Desarrollo. Revista Latinoamericana de Economia.* Vol. 11, No. 44. Retrieved from: https://www.probdes.iiec.unam.mx/index.php/pde/article/view/37413

Medina Gonzalez-Davila, J. (Summer, 2015). "Mexican Intelligence". *The Intelligencer. Journal of U.S. Intelligence Studies.* Vol. 21, No. 2. Retrieved from: https://www.afio.com/publications/MEDINA%20Mexican%20Intelligence%202015%20Sep%2001%20FINAL.pdf

Mexico Center/International Law Section of the Texas State Bar Association. (March 29, 2019). *Security and Justice in Mexico.* (Panel Discussion: Carlos Bravo-Regidor). Baker Institute, Rice University. Retrieved from: https://www.bakerinstitute.org/events/1996/

Mexico. Presidencia de la Republica. (2014). *Programa para la Seguridad Nacional 2014–2018. Una Política Multidimensional para Mexico en el Siglo XXI.* Consejo de Seguridad Nacional. Retrieved from: https://www.resdal.org/caeef-resdal/assets/mexico----programa-para-la-seguridad-nacional.pdf

Moloeznik, M. P. (July-December, 2019). "Seguridad Interior, un Concepto Ambiguo". *Revista del Instituto de Ciencias Juridicas de Puebla.* Nueva Epoca. Vol. 13, No. 44. Retrieved from: http://www.scielo.org.mx/pdf/rius/v13n44/1870-2147-rius-13-44-147.pdf

Navarro, A. W. (2010). *Political Intelligence and the Creation of Modern Mexico, 1938–1954.* University Park: Pennsylvania State University Press.

Piñeyro, J. L. (October/December, 1994). "La Seguridad Nacional con Salinas de Gortari". *Foro Internacional.* Vol. XXXIV, No. 4, 759, 760–769.

Piñeyro, J. L. (October/December, 2001). "La Seguridad Nacional con Zedillo". *Foro Internacional.* Vol. XLI, No. 4, 940, 955.

Reuter, P., and Ronfeldt, D. (Fall, 1992). "Quest for Integrity: The Mexican–U.S. Drug Trade in the 1980s". *Journal of Interamerican Studies and World Affairs.* Vol. 34, No. 3, 105.

Rodriguez-Castañeda, R. (2013). *El Policía. Perseguía, torturaba, mataba.* México, DF: Editorial Grijalvo.

Semple, K. (June 14, 2019). "Mexico's National Guard, a 'Work in Progress,' Deployed to Curb Migration". *The New York Times.* Retrieved from: https://www.nytimes.com/2019/06/14/world/americas/mexico-migration-national-guard.html

Speck, M. (February 26, 2019). "Great Expectations and Grim Realities in AMLO's Mexico". *PRISM.* Vol. 8, No. 1. Retrieved from: https://cco.ndu.edu/Portals/96/Documents/prism/prism8_1/190306_PRISM8_1_Speck.pdf?ver=2019-03-05-153005-517

Tirado, E. (March 8, 2020). "AMLO y Ejercito: La Traicion Civilista". *Proceso.* Retrieved from: https://www.proceso.com.mx/620802/amlo-y-ejercito-la-traicion-civilista

US General Accounting Office (GAO). (June 12, 1996). *Drug Control. Counternarcotics Efforts in Mexico.* Report to Congressional Requesters. National Security and International Affairs Division, GAO/NSIAD-96–163. Washington, DC.

Valdes, G. (November 21, 2018). "Plan de Seguridad: Cuatro Fallas". *Milenio.* Retrieved from: https://www.milenio.com/opinion/guillermo-valdes-castellanos/doble-mirada/plan-de-seguridad-cuatro-fallas

Vignettes, M. (May 9, 2019). "Mexico's Intelligence Community. A Critical Description". *International Journal of Intelligence and Counterintelligence.* Vol. 32, No. 2. Retrieved from: https://www.tandfonline.com/doi/full/10.1080/08850607.2018.1522227?af=R&

The White House. (February, 1998). *United States/Mexico Bi-National Drug Strategy.* Office of National Drug Control Policy (ONDCP). Washington, DC: Government Printing Office.

4 Execution

How National Security Is Implemented?

4.1 Structure

This chapter describes the implementation of national security in Mexico. In the context of a strong presidential system, the basis of the national security structure in the country has been, at least since 1988, either the National Security Cabinet or the National Security Council, which have been kept as purely deliberative bodies. In Mexico, the guidelines for a National Security System have been already established since 2009 through the National Security Programs describing the roles of the different agencies participating in the national security decision-making process, and the challenge, therefore, is not the absence of a framework, but the lack of political will and long-term vision to make the system work. Drug trafficking represents a complication for Mexico's security because of its transformation, from a health issue to a public security matter, into a national security threat, in the process mixing the coercive instruments of the state to the point where the military, a national security instrument par excellence to deter foreign threats, has been deployed to the streets to deal with organized crime on the country's urban and rural areas, without effectively containing the challenge.

Once the military was separated from politics in Mexico by the 1940s, civilians remained in charge of managing what could be considered "national security" affairs. The first civilian institutions created in this field were those with intelligence responsibilities whose main objective was to protect and provide the president with information on domestic challenges. These were the organizations that preceded the CISEN (currently the National Intelligence Center-CNI), and from the very beginning they were under SEGOB.

The main institution implementing national security in Mexico was the National Security Cabinet – one of a series of "specialized cabinets" – which was created by decree for the first time on December

7, 1988 within the Office of Coordination of the Presidency, to manage national security activities. Article 4, Section V established that the cabinet was to be integrated by SEGOB, SRE, SEDENA, SEMAR, and PGR (DOF 1988). Its creation was in line with the modernization process started by President Salinas, not only in the economic sphere, but also in several policy areas, even though there were several contradictions. For instance, coordination of national security remained in fact as a purview of SEGOB, and regarding the definition of national security as the "integral development of the country", the National Security Cabinet did not include any agency in charge of promoting development, as it could be expected (Aguayo 1991: 95–6).

This cabinet continued to operate under President Zedillo, and at the beginning of the Fox Administration, it was replaced by a National Security Council (CSN) headed, for the first time ever, by a National Security Adviser. Because of inter-bureaucratic disagreements, a year after being designated, the Adviser was appointed Mexico's Representative to the UN and, for all practical purposes, this position ceased to exist, leaving therefore a void. Even though the creation of a CSN was a step in the right direction for the design of a comprehensive and long-term national security policy, just as in the case of its predecessors – the National Security Cabinet – the CSN never had a permanent staff but continued only as a deliberative instance for the coordination and adoption of agreements and resolutions. This body was, nevertheless, the beginning of an integrative process that would have allowed the government to have a greater capacity for anticipation, although not necessarily reaction, regarding international developments. As correctly pointed out by an observer,

> definitely Mexico will not be able to fully develop an active and independent foreign policy as long as it does not reduce its external vulnerability. It is important to understand that the implementation of any foreign policy requires, besides interest and political will for its execution, the ability or the power to instrument it.
>
> (Santos-Camaal 1985: 26)

In 2003, after the National Security Adviser left for the UN, the National Security Cabinet was reactivated as an institution "in charge of analysis, definition, coordination, monitoring and assessment of policies, strategies and actions of the Federal Public Administration on national security" (DOF 2003). Compared to the previous cabinet, it added as its members Public Security, Treasury, Public Administration and CISEN – as Executive Secretary – and PGR, and eliminated the position of National Security Adviser established on January 8, 2001.

The CSN was again restored by the LSN, Title 2, Chapter 1, Article 12, in order "to coordinate actions to preserve national security", designating SEGOB as its Executive Secretary, and a Technical Secretary appointed by the President (Camara de Diputados 2019a). Despite being established by law, the government of President Calderon worked through a National Security Cabinet, although there was a National Public Security Council that concentrated on public security matters. President Peña-Nieto revived the CSN, and AMLO currently works with a cabinet despite the fact that his PND establishes that the CSN has to execute the National Security Program (Camara de Diputados 2019b: 22).

What is important to underline is the fact that by simply maintaining a deliberative body, there is no capacity at the highest echelon of the Mexican government to generate a long-term perspective or an integral vision about the impact of foreign developments on Mexico's national security, for which the country is only reactive. Mexico's increasing international exposure requires a CSN with a permanent team working on both specialized issues and areas of the globe, in order to advise the President in a timely manner and to inform the decision-making process.

4.2 Process

As already mentioned, the guiding document of the Executive branch in Mexico is each administration's PND, which establishes the objectives and strategies of the government, in turn. This document is required by Article 26 of the Constitution, and in accordance with Articles 9 and 22 to 42 of the Organic Law of the Federal Public Administration (Camara de Diputados 2020). As stated by the Planning Law, there is a National Democratic Planning System where the Planning Units of each federal department concur, which are, in turn, coordinated by the Secretary of the Treasury that incorporates the proposals of the different sectors of society (Camara de Diputados 2018). This is the basis, in turn, for the design of each of the agencies' programs, including those participating in national security.

As previously noted, what is known in Mexico as "national security" is an issue that has been mainly coordinated by SEGOB, even though on paper, guidelines have assigned this task to the National Security Cabinets and the CSN. However, SEGOB has been the Executive Secretary on both deliberative bodies, and it is from these instances where the directives have come from to implement national security measures. Under AMLO, SEGOB has been stripped off of its security responsibilities by being transferred to the newly created SSPC, keeping only some responsibilities such as immigration policy, human rights, and emergency management.

A significant advance in the process of implementing national security actions was the 2006 decree regarding the "Regulations for the Coordination of Executive Actions on National Security Matters", which establishes criteria and procedures for coordination of activities in this field. It is up to the Executive Secretary to promote coordination. According to the document, the Executive Secretary and the Technical Secretary will address national security issues with a strategic and comprehensive view regarding two aspects: (a) public policies; and (b) strategic intelligence (DOF 2006). Article 6 with respect to the former establishes that the Technical Secretary will propose to the CSN the policies, guidelines, and actions. Article 7 regarding the latter, on the other hand, indicates that it will have as its objective the generation of knowledge for decision-making and the execution of strategic projects, guaranteeing the secure generation of data to deactivate threats (DOF 2006).

It is important to note that both aspects are aimed at safeguarding national security interests, and to guide both the PND and the National Security Program's strategic proposals and lines of action that are submitted to the CSN for consideration. The program then defines the response to national security issues through a comprehensive process that includes several aspects: the President making decisions after consideration by the CSN; the integration of strategic intelligence that is CISEN's responsibility to support the decision-making process; the promotion of public policies that include the execution and follow-up of CSN agreements by the Technical Secretary; emergency planning and management, and security operations; and protection of the process that consists in control and surveillance mechanisms in charge of the Executive Secretary through CISEN (DOF 2006). CISEN's strategic intelligence duty consists in preparing the National Risk Agenda (ANR) that, as an annual intelligence product, is a prospective document that identifies risks and threats, and guides intelligence activities. The ANR is approved by the President at the CSN, as proposed by the Technical Secretary (CISEN 2014).

Article 8 of the Regulations establishes that national security decisions "must be supported by intelligence processes", while Article 20 indicates that the execution of the national security policy will be conducted within the CSN based on the PND, the National Security

Program, the ANR, the Strategic Action Plan, and the operational programs. The Executive Secretary shall submit the reports and programs to the CSN, as well as to the Bicameral Commission, prior to CSN authorization. Likewise, Article 21 indicates that the Executive Secretary may propose to the CSN the formation of Specialized Committees to address the agenda's issues, with CISEN as the Chair of the Committees that are formed (DOF 2006).

After the bases were established in the Regulations, the first time in history the government made public a National Security Program was that of 2009–2012, as anticipated in President Calderon's 2007–2012 PND (DOF 2009). The Program is conceived as an instrument to guide the government's efforts to preserve national security through the establishment of a system, which is a significant advance over previous efforts; in fact, one of the elements that keeps the execution of the policy within the CSN is the program itself (DOF 2009).

The program represents a qualitative change in the implementation of national security, in the sense of presenting the evolution of security and a diagnosis of risks and threats, the legal framework, and especially the foundation for a National Security System that includes the components already mentioned in the Regulations. It adds that the execution of national security actions is the responsibility of the national security instances – that are the operative tools of the system in charge of materializing the lines of action – which also coordinate activities with autonomous agencies, state governments, and municipalities (DOF 2009).

The same document points out that the formal articulation of the system is relatively recent in the life of the Mexican state, and that it was until 2005 when it was made explicit in the LSN, although it recognizes that there is a gap between what the system is and what it produces, and what it should be and what it actually generates. As an example of self-criticism, it states that it requires "to start from a critical understanding of reality and to deepen the characterization of each risk and threat", and "to operate based on a more comprehensive approach to the set of threats and risks so that it reaches a greater coherence in its approach" (DOF 2009).

The second of the National Security Programs, that for 2014–2018, was presented by President Peña-Nieto. It was a program based on a series of meetings proceedings' compilation in which members of government postgraduate schools related to national security, such as CODENAL, CESNAV, the School of Intelligence for National Security (ESISEN), and the Matias Romero Institute for Diplomatic Studies (IMRED), participated. It was described as an "unprecedented exercise", having summoned scholars, analysts, and authorities of these institutions so that, in a variety of sessions, the instruments of public policy that make up the program were defined (Mexico 2014: 9–18).

This is a document that builds on its predecessor and, as such, also describes the legal and conceptual framework, as well as Mexico's strategic environment. The new aspect is that it adopts a "multidimensional" security policy (Mexico 2014: 27), as well as a national security agenda for the future, which contributed to the incremental steps necessary for the development of a more comprehensive and long-term vision for the country.

Adopting a multidimensional approach and recognizing the impact of trends and factors that influence Mexico's national interests, it establishes that the government has two major strategic objectives: consolidating the National Security System; and ensuring that national security policy has a multidimensional perspective (Mexico 2014: 32). To achieve these goals, a National Intelligence System would be developed to support the CSN deliberation process. It then addresses the fundamentals, challenges, objectives, and an agenda for the future.

The "Mexico in Peace" objective of Peña-Nieto's PND required a comprehensive national security policy based on a "multidimensional" orientation, in line with the Organization of American States (OAS) vision on the subject (see Blackwell 2015), while the legal foundations were the LSN and the plan derived from the PND, in both aspects already mentioned, public policies, and strategic intelligence.

The second program was more specific than the previous one and pointed out that the national security approach proposed by the administration had three strategic objectives: to consolidate a National Security System, to build a National Intelligence System, and to develop a Culture of National Security (Mexico 2014: 37–43). The Culture of National Security objective requires dialogue and coordination with political actors, the private sector, and academia and civil society to strengthen the democratic regime, since a state policy on the matter cannot prosper without the participation of the society. It is necessary for society to know the ends and instruments of national security in order to build trust and credibility (Mexico 2014: 42). Even though the government proposes to democratize national security decision-making through the promotion of a Culture of National Security, the need for more democratic practices in this field is an idea that has been on the table for some time (Aguayo 1991: 101), but it was until recently that it became an official objective.

Very interesting, the second program makes a more extensive evaluation of the factors of national power and of Mexico's position in the world as an "emerging power", and with respect to other regions, as well as in the multilateral sphere (Mexico 2014: 48–54). It includes, however, an internal security section and recognizes the penetration of institutions by organized crime and the fact that it has ceased to be an internal security challenge to become a national security one (Mexico 2014: 55–60). It proposes addressing cyber risks and the southern border, and provides a glossary of terms. On the agenda for the future, reference is made to four challenges: preservation of biodiversity as a strategic resource; impact of climate change on food security and access to water; transformation of the global energy landscape and energy security; and management of health and pandemic resources in a scenario of global openness (Mexico 2014: 62–6).

One relevant finding from the aforementioned review is that Mexico does not lack the foundations to transform security because a National Security System, in fact, already exists, albeit on paper; it rather lacks the political will to carry out the necessary changes, which is a contradictory posture because the same governments that have favored Mexico's opening, including AMLO with the negotiation of the Agreement between the United States of America, the United Mexican States, and Canada (USMCA), are the ones who have fallen short in making the changes the country requires. Restructuring national security is a process AMLO should have built on, instead of once again starting from scratch at the beginning of each administration, which does not contribute to the consolidation of a state policy on this matter.

4.3 Second Complication: Drug Trafficking

This subsection explains that the lack of a clear distinction in Mexico among national, internal, and public security is related not only to the legal overlapping where national security includes internal security, but also to the fact that drugs – a health problem in the first place – went from a public security matter to become a national security threat to be dealt with the coercive instruments of the state, in particular by deploying the military to the streets, thus creating an evident mix-up regarding the instruments to address specific security challenges.

Drug trafficking, in turn, cannot be understood without reference to geography, in particular to Mexico's vicinity to the United States. The presence of drug trafficking in the US-Mexico bilateral agenda is a predictable situation in a part of the globe where an industrialized nation, which happens to be the world's largest drug market, shares a long and permeable border with a developing neighbor that is also a significant drug producer and transit point.

Even though drug trafficking is a trans-national challenge not restricted to US-Mexican relations, it is an issue with a long history in the bilateral agenda that has been characterized by cooperation but more often by conflict. If it is true that Mexico has contributed to US counterdrug efforts, US drug policy toward its southern neighbor has been described as "cyclical in nature, often unilateral, incident-prone and highly contentious" (Craig 1989: 78). The prevalent view in Mexico regarding drugs is that the origin of the problem has been US demand. This viewpoint has not been unique to Mexican analysts. For instance, according to a US scholar,

> The fundamental source of the drug problem, of *narcotrafico* in the Americas, is the presence of and power of consumer demand. Demand for drugs is most conspicuous in advanced industrial countries, in Europe, and –especially important for Latin America- in the United States. Demand is what creates the market for drugs. So long as demand continues, there will be people engaged in supply.
> (Smith 1992: 2)

The dominant US view has been that at the center of this issue has been Mexican pervasive corruption, as it will be discussed in more detail below.

The bilateral management of the issue, nevertheless, has been defined mainly in US terms, reflecting the asymmetry of power between the two countries and the resulting unbalanced approach. An additional factor complicating a coordinated response to the problem has been "the overtly political treatment of the drug problem" (Gonzalez 1989: 1) in the United States. The negative connotation for politicians to appear "soft on drugs", on the one hand, and the aversion to the consequences of fighting drugs in terms of violence within its own territory, on the other hand, have limited available options to deal with the problem in the United States. As a result of these constraints, the United States has basically exported abroad the costs of fighting drugs. The US supply-side approach, nevertheless, has proved to be ineffective so far, by "[failing] to view the drug market as an integrated market" (Del Villar 1989: 94), requiring, therefore, a comprehensive response.

Notwithstanding general agreement on the relevance of demand in determining the phenomenon, Mexico has for long cooperated with US anti-drug efforts. In fact, it is considered that "Mexico may represent the 'end case', in terms of what the United States can reasonably expect from efforts at drug control within the context of continued US demand" (Reuter and Ronfeldt 1992: 90). It is important to note, however, that while the "dealing with supply" argument has been politically convenient in the United States, it has not contributed to a long-term solution of the problem. In the specific case of Mexico, the US supply-oriented strategy and the transfer of drug-consumption costs abroad have resulted in the militarization of anti-drug policies that have only led to higher levels of violence, human rights abuses, and the armed forces' exposure to corruption without significantly dealing with the problem.

The US government has consistently "encouraged" Mexico to deal with drug production and trafficking, and Mexican authorities have responded in order to contain US pressure, but also because of the need to avoid criminal organizations to take control of areas and institutions of the country. Nevertheless, Mexico's anti-drug activities have failed so far to stem the flow of drugs into the United States not only because of the persistence of US demand, but also because of the existence of corruption within its security organizations.

For instance, as a response to US pressure, in the 1980s, the Mexican government recognized drug trafficking to pose a threat to Mexico's society and institutions, and set out to reform its security apparatus. While Mexican authorities had traditionally avoided identifying drugs as a national security threat in order to prevent the United States from using this designation to justify interventionist policies, President de la Madrid eventually echoed President Ronald Reagan by declaring that drug trafficking should be considered a threat to national security (Doyle 1993:84). In response to raising political pressures in anticipation of the November 1986 mid-term elections, President Reagan set the stage for a further expansion of the US military's participation in drug control. On April 8, 1986, he issued National Security Decision Directive No. 221 (NSC-NSDD-221) "Narcotics and National Security", which established that "the expanding scope of global narcotics trafficking has created a situation which today adds another significant dimension to the law enforcement and public health aspects of this international problem and *threatens the national security of the United States*" (White House 1986: 1).

President Salinas, de la Madrid's successor, reasserted the previous administration's declaration that drug trafficking represented a national security threat:

> The fight against drugs is a high priority in my government for three fundamental reasons: because it constitutes an assault on

> the health of Mexico's citizens, because it promises to affect Mexican national security, and finally, because the community of nations must stand together on this issue.
>
> (Quoted by Reuter and Ronfeldt 1992: 110)

In contrast to the United States where the definition of drug trafficking as a national security issue helped to justify the military's support to LEAs in the "war on drugs", in Mexico, the definition did not have the same purpose because the military has been already involved in anti-drug missions. Instead, it allowed the Mexican government to portray the fight against drugs to be in the interest of the country, and not only in that of the United States. This declaration had a political objective which was "[to provide] the base for rallying new political support for an increasingly expensive, difficult, and controversial effort" (Reuter and Ronfeldt 1992: 115).

In this context, the task for the Salinas Administration consisted not only in confronting more capable drug organizations within Mexico, but also showing the United States the determination of the new government in its fight against drugs (Andreas 2000: 53). One important aspect of drug control in Mexico during the Salinas government was the increasing participation of the armed forces, which was reflected in the fact that "about one-third of the military's budget was devoted to that effort by the end of the 1980s" (Andreas 2000: 55).

In general terms, the US and Mexican response to the continued failures of interdiction has been the intensification of coercive measures. After taking office in December 1994, President Zedillo declared that drug trafficking was "Mexico's number one security threat", as mentioned earlier. The fact that the situation had not improved in comparison to previous Mexican administrations was evident in the US Department of State's reports covering 1991–1997. They established that Mexico was the origin of the majority of drugs entering the US illegal market (between 20% and 30% of heroin, 80% of marijuana, 80% of synthetic drugs, and the platform for 50–60% of cocaine from South America) (Storrs 1998: 2–3).

President Zedillo's response to continuing corruption in Mexico was to turn once again to the military. In late 1995, the armed forces increasingly took over several state police departments, and coordination for public security increased among the military, state, and local police (Schulz 1997: 2). The intensified participation of the Mexican military in anti-drug activities, however, did not produce a significant change. Comparison between President Salinas' last three years and President Zedillo's first three years shows more continuity than change in the pattern of aggressive drug enforcement (Storrs 1998: 4), without significantly disrupting the flow of drugs.

The increasing involvement of the Mexican military in drug control operations confronted the already mentioned predicament of greater exposition to corruption. Within the wider issue of anti-drug operations, one of the most sensitive aspects for the bilateral relationship has been the way in which the drug trade has corrupted Mexican authorities. This corruption, which has taken many forms and has occurred at different levels, has often complicated the process of forging a bilateral response to the drug trafficking threat. Reuter and Ronfeldt point out that the United States has been led to more aggressive postures, "not so much by the extent of drug flows from Mexico as by the perception that the Mexican control efforts are corrupt", and they add, "the Mexican drug problem, as it affects bilateral relations with the United States, is essentially an issue of integrity" (Reuter and Ronfeldt 1992: 131). In the most recent drug corruption case on the Mexican side, the Secretary of Public Security under ex-President Calderon was indicted in a New York Court under charges of working for the Sinaloa cartel (Feuer 2091).

By militarizing the response to a pervasive problem such as drug trafficking, as this course of action basically continued under subsequent administrations, Mexico has employed a national security instrument, the armed forces, to attack a health and a public security issue, in the first place, confusing in the process the instruments to address national, and internal, security issues, without achieving any meaningful results.

Bibliography

Aguayo, S. (1991). "Un Concepto de Seguridad Nacional Mexicana para la Decada de los Noventa". In R. Roett (Ed.), *Relaciones Exteriores de Mexico en la Decada de los Noventa* (pp. 95, 96, 101). Mexico: Siglo XXI Editores.

Andreas, P. R. (2000). *Border Games. Policing the U.S.-Mexico Divide*. Cornell Studies in Political Economy. Edited by Peter J. Katzenstein. Ithaca, NY: Cornell University Press.

Blackwell, A. (April, 2015). *10 Years of Multidimensional Security*. Latin America Program. Wilson Center. Retrieved from: https://adamblackwell.files.wordpress.com/2015/06/10-years-of-multidimensional-security.pdf

Camara de Diputados del H. Congreso de la Union. (January 22, 2020). *Ley Organica de la Administracion Publica Federal*. Nueva Ley publicada en el Diario Oficial de la Federacion el 29 de diciembre de 1976. Retrieved from: http://www.diputados.gob.mx/LeyesBiblio/pdf/153_220120.pdf

Camara de Diputados del H. Congreso de la Union. (February 16, 2018). *Ley de Planeacion.* Nueva Ley publicada en el Diario Oficial de la Federacion el 5 de enero de 1983. Retrieved from: http://www.diputados.gob.mx/LeyesBiblio/pdf/59_160218.pdf

Camara de Diputados del H. Congreso de la Union. (November 8, 2019a). *Ley de Seguridad Nacional.* Nueva Ley publicada en el Diario Oficial de la Federación el 31 de enero de 2005. Retrieved from: http://www.diputados.gob.mx/LeyesBiblio/pdf/LSegNac_081119.pdf

Camara de Diputados. LXIV Legislatura. (April 30, 2019b). *Plan Nacional de Desarrollo 2019–2024.* Gaceta Parlamentaria. Año XX. Número 5266-XVIII. Retrieved from: http://gaceta.diputados.gob.mx/PDF/64/2019/abr/20190430-XVIII.pdf

CISEN. (December 19, 2014). "Seguridad Nacional". SEGOB. Retrieved from: http://www.cisen.gob.mx/snSegNal.html

Craig, R. B. (1989). "US Narcotics Policy toward Mexico: Consequences for the Bilateral Relationship". In G. Gonzalez and M. Tienda (Eds.), *The Drug Connection in US-Mexican Relations* (p. 78). Dimensions of US-Mexican Relations. Vol. 4. Papers prepared for the Bilateral Commission on the Future of United States-Mexican Relations. Center for US-Mexican Studies, University of California, San Diego.

Del Villar, S. I. (1989). "Controlling the US-Mexican Drug Market". In Gonzlez and Tienda. *Drug Connection*, 94.

Diario Oficial de la Federacion (DOF). (April 9, 2003). *Acuerdo por el que se Crea el Gabinete de Seguridad Nacional.* Retrieved from: http://dof.gob.mx/nota_detalle.php?codigo=2045345&fecha=09/04/2003

Diario Oficial de la Federacion (DOF). (December 7, 1988). *Acuerdo por el que se Crea la Oficina de Coordinación de la Presidencia de la República.* Retrieved from: http://dof.gob.mx/nota_detalle.php?codigo=4794890&fecha=07/12/1988

Diario Oficial de la Federacion (DOF). (August 20, 2009). *Decreto por el que se Publica el Programa para la Seguridad Nacional 2009–2014.* Retrieved from: http://www.cns.gob.mx/portalWebApp/ShowBinary?nodeId=/BEA%20Repository/578170//archivo

Diario Oficial de la Federacion (DOF). (November 29, 2006). *Reglamento para la Coordinacion de Acciones Ejecutivas en Materia de Seguridad Nacional.* Retrieved from: http://www.diputados.gob.mx/LeyesBiblio/regla/n18.pdf

Doyle, K. (February, 1993). "The Militarization of the Drug War in Mexico". *Current History.* Vol. 92, No. 571, 84.

Feuer, A. (December 10, 2019). "Architect of Mexico's War on Cartels Is Accused of Taking Bribes from One". *The New York Times.* Retrieved from: https://www.nytimes.com/2019/12/10/world/americas/genaro-garcia-luna-mexico-arrest.html

Gonzalez, G. (1989). "The Drug Connection in U.S.-Mexican Relations: Introduction". In Gonzalez and Tienda. *Drug Connection*, 1.

Mexico. Presidencia de la Republica. (2014). *Programa para la Seguridad Nacional 2014–2018. Una Política Multidimensional para Mexico en el Siglo*

XXI. Consejo de Seguridad Nacional. Retrieved from: https://www.resdal.org/caeef-resdal/assets/mexico----programa-para-la-seguridad-nacional.pdf

Reuter, P., and Ronfeldt, D. (Fall, 1992). "Quest for Integrity: The Mexican-U.S. Drug Trade in the 1980s". *Journal of Interamerican Studies and World Affairs.* Vol. 34, No. 3, 90, 110, 115, 131.

Santos-Camaal, M. (1985). "Mexico frente a Centroamerica: Un concepto estrategico nacional en acción". *Revista del CESNAV.* Vol. 51, 26.

Schulz, D. E. (June, 1997). *Between Rock and a Hard Place: The United States, Mexico, and the Agony of National Security.* U.S. Army War College. Carlisle, PA: Strategic Studies Institute. Retrieved from: http://carlisle-www.army.mil/usassi/ssipubs/pubs97/

Smith, P. H. (1992). "The Political Economy of Drugs: Conceptual Issues and Policy Options". In P. H. Smith. (Ed.), *Drug Policy in the Americas.* Boulder, CO: Westview Press, Inc, 2.

Storrs, K. L. Specialist on Latin American Affairs. (March, 1998). "Mexico's Counter-Narcotics Efforts under Zedillo, December 1994 to March 1998". *CRS Report to Congress.* Foreign Affairs and National Defense Division, Received through the CRS Web, 98–161F. Updated March 4, 1998. Congressional Research Service (CRS). Washington, DC: The Library of Congress.

The White House. (April 8, 1986). "Narcotics and National Security". National Security Decision Directive Number 221 (NSC362-NSDD-221). In NSDD – National Security Decision Directives, Reagan Administration. Federation of American Scientists (FAS). Intelligence Resource Programs. Retrieved from: http://www.fas.org/irp/offdocs/nsdd/nsdd-221.htm

5 A Complex Security Context and the Reasons for Change

5.1 Domestic Challenges

This chapter discusses drug-related violence as the most pressing domestic security challenge in Mexico. A review of President Calderon's period is carried out as key to understanding a turning point in the country in terms of the fragmentation of criminal groups and dispersion of illicit activities, as the main characteristic of the current security context. Analysis then turns to Mexico's increasing external exposure as a result not only of its accession to NAFTA, but also because of the diversification of its trade networks and increasing multilateral political activism in the context of globalization. In order to face both its domestic and external security environments, the end of the chapter addresses different aspects to guide security reform based on a correct understanding of the nature of the national security concept.

Mexico's most relevant national security challenge is the high level of violence generated by drug trafficking in the last decades. This is also the most pressing domestic problem linked to the exterior, as it is a transnational issue more than a home-grown problem. The common narrative in the last years has been that the origin of high-level violence in Mexico was the "Calderon war", the offensive launched by the former president starting in 2006, but the explanation is more complex than that. The Calderon Administration, however, is key to understanding the current security situation because of its impact on the multiplication of drug trafficking groups.

As President Calderon's term came to an end on the last day of November 2012, Mexico was facing a complex security situation as drug trafficking organizations (DTOs) were engaged in a violent competition for dominance of the lucrative corridors to the United States. According to the *National Drug Control Assessment 2011*, Mexican DTOs were preeminent in the drug trade because of "their control of smuggling routes across the US Southwest border and their capacity to produce, transport, and/or distribute cocaine, heroin, marijuana, and methamphetamine" (USDOJ 2011: 2). It was established that "Mexican DTOs represent the greatest organized crime threat to the United States" (USDOJ 2008: iii).

Notwithstanding the fact that President Calderon intensified the fight against drug trafficking in Mexico since assuming power on December 1, 2006, the security context in the country began to deteriorate long before, as the trend of violent deaths in Mexico – at the time had already numbered in excess of thousand a year – had been gradually increasing in the 2000s (Astorga and Shirk 2010: 41).

An interesting argument locates the origin of high drug violence in Mexico in 2001, as a result of the Mexican government's offensive against the vicious Arellano-Felix organization (AFO/Tijuana DTO), which, in turn, ended up strengthening the Sinaloa group, whetting thus its appetite for a greater share of the drug market (Felbab-Brown 2009: 5). Violence in Mexico, however, is a multifaceted phenomenon and there are four general factors that help explain this context.

First, recurrent economic crises in Mexico between the 1970s and 1990s, and consequent economic neo-liberal reforms since the mid-1980s significantly eroded standards of living in the country. Besides increasing unemployment, the situation contributed to the growth of the underground economy, which by some estimates provided income for 28.4 million people or 64.01% of Mexico's economically active population (Monroy 2011). Currently, this figure is 56.7% of the workforce (Garcia 2019).

Second, the shift of South American cocaine routes from the Caribbean to continental Mexico in the second half of the 1980s, after US authorities closed that basin's aerial and maritime corridors (with the creation of Joint Task Force No. 4 [JTF-4] in Key West, Florida), resulted in a more prominent role for Mexican DTOs by eventually increasing both their profits and power, as Colombia's cartels (i.e. Medellin and Cali) also became gradually weakened by joint US-Colombia law enforcement action (Beittel 2011: 5). It is estimated that drug trafficking generated around $30 billion dollars a year for Mexican DTOs – equivalent to between 3% and 4% of Mexico's GDP ($1.5 trillion) – in the process providing means of subsistence for close to half a million people (Shirk 2011: 7).

Third, while these law enforcement and economic changes were taking place, political alternation in Mexico, especially as the PRI lost the Presidency to the PAN in 2000, eroded the traditional social control mechanisms of the single-party political system, thus weakening the official containment approach that allowed drug cartels to grow with the connivance and protection of authorities that also prevented violent confrontations among these groups. This reallocation of power contributed to the already mentioned political fragmentation and dislocation of centrally planned security policies, resulting in greater DTO's autonomy (Cerda-Ardura 2011). The fact that the government's response to drug trafficking in Mexico became fragmented because of the shift described earlier, that is, that either the level of response to crime or the level of complicity with crime varied for authorities in different areas of the country, in part explains why President Calderon's security efforts were not successful in dealing with both drug flows and violent incidents (Cerda-Ardura 2011). The lesson from this is that in the long run, a comprehensive political agreement in Mexico is required in order to effectively contain violence in the country.

Fourth, as a result of political change and transformations in law enforcement agencies in Mexico, especially the abolition of the DFS (the DTOs arbitrator) in response to US pressure after the Camarena assassination, the DTOs bipolar structure began to crumble (at that time, the two main DTOs were Sinaloa and Golfo), leading to the accession of new leaders within the fractionalized groups and also to a more intense competition among them.

By the 1990s, there were four major DTOs in Mexico, in comparison to more recent years when it has been possible to identify at least six groups (an intelligence document prepared at the end of the Peña-Nieto Administration established that there were 6 big cartels and more than 80 cells operating in the 32 states [Infobae 2019]). The country thus found itself with the worst of the two worlds: less official control over these criminal groups because of political fragmentation, and less respect for the traditional rules of the game on the part of the new leaders of these organizations. According to a perspective, the "self-destructive" process that contributes to the breakup of these groups, that is, the violent methods used to settle disputes among them, at the same time compels them to incorporate new members from marginalized sectors of society whose inexperience and, sometimes, greed, in turn, lead to more violence (Villalobos 2010), and this is an argument that helps explain why the current organizations are less respectful than the old ones of what used to be the "non-written" rules of the game (i.e. no violence on the streets).

By the 1990s, moreover, the Gulf organization co-opted members of the Mexican Army Air/Amphibious Special Forces Unit (GAFES/GANFES) who became known as "Zetas" (see Grayson 2015), and this development resulted in the introduction, for the first time, of paramilitary tactics in the confrontation among DTOs; they implied not only the presence, but also the control of criminal activities within a given territorial demarcation by these groups, and this eventually led to confrontation with the government after these organizations were taking over exclusive functions of the state (Cerda-Ardura 2011), such as challenging the official monopoly of the use of force. In this context, and in comparison with previous periods of violence, DTOs' behavior has been characterized by their aggression against the upper echelons of security forces; the brazenness of their brutal acts; and the use of high-power weapons (i.e. AK-47s, MP-5s, AR-15s, P90s, submachine guns, grenade launchers, and .50 caliber machine guns) (Gereben Schaefer, Bahney and Riley 2009: xiv).

President Calderon responded to this situation by escalating the fight against DTOs, increasingly involving the military in regional operations around the country to contain violence generated by competition among these groups, that is, by further militarizing the response to organized crime activities. This course of action, however, was not new in Mexico as a measure of last resort in response to widespread corruption among its police forces, notwithstanding that the military had not proved to be above and beyond drug-related corruption.

The centerpiece of the Calderon administration's strategy focused on the idea of turning a "national security" problem into a "public safety" challenge by breaking down the big DTOs into smaller groups, under the logic that smaller factions are more amenable to be contained (Shirk 2011: 9). This strategy put a premium on neutralizing high-value targets (HVTs), and this orientation contributed to intra-cartel conflict (Salmeron 2006; Rawlins 2011: 4). In fact, decapitating DTOs created more chaos and uncertainty in the short-term without necessarily dealing with either drug distribution or internal violence. This strategy was also criticized in terms of an offensive that was launched without previously having the required tools to get the job done, evident, for instance, in the fact that not only Mexico's police forces were characterized by their lack of professionalism and ingrained corruption (O'Neil 2010: 70), but also, according to an estimation, by the fact that only 1 or 2 per 100 crimes actually ended up in conviction, which provides the picture of the serious level of impunity in the country and the long way Mexico still has to go to achieve an effective judicial reform (Shirk 2011: 11). According to a 2017 analysis on Mexico's judicial system, the country's average impunity index (cases known by the authority not receiving a satisfactory response) is 87.3% (Mexico Evalua 2018: 104).

It is important to note that even though violence in Mexico has been localized, it has spread internally in the last years. A 2011 study points out that 2/3 of drug-related deaths occurred in just 5 of the 32 states, and around 80% of them occurred in 168 of the country's 2,456 municipalities, even though the density of violence in some locations such as Ciudad Juarez was significant at the time (Shirk 2011: 8), which was reflected in the 3,096 murders that occurred there just in 2010 (Felbab-Brown 2011: 8). More recently, 5 states in Mexico (Colima 93; Baja California 89.1; Guerrero 68.1; Chihuahua 58.7; and Guanajuato 53.8) have the highest number of homicides per 100 thousand habitants (Zepeda-Lecuona 2019).

The Mexican government at the time might have been correct in believing that the atomization of DTOs and disorder in the drug market indicated that anti-narcotics operations were effective, but the other side of the coin is that authorities found it difficult to contain crime (Felbab-Brown 2011: 11). One reason for this unsatisfactory outcome was that unlike Colombia in the 1980s and early 1990s, the greater number of DTOs in Mexico made it difficult for law enforcement agencies to identify with accuracy the perpetrators of crime (Felbab-Brown 2011: 40). It is important to note that, according to a contrasting perspective, if it is true that DTOs' fragmentation brought with it negative consequences (i.e. an increase of violence), these effects were thought to be temporary and part of an inevitable step to improve security in the long-term (Villalobos 2012: 5). Whether atomizing DTOs was a sensible course of action or not, it is important to note that dealing with common crime in the country requires to deal first with organized crime because of the fact that illegal activities such as kidnapping and extortion and, more recently, fuel theft – apparently unrelated to drugs – are in fact elements of the DTOs' strategy to maintain management of crime in the *plaza*. Moreover, the need for consolidating regional influence has been a direct consequence of the growth of *narco-menudeo* (retail drug sales on the streets) in Mexico since the mid-1990s (Calderon 2010: 2).

The United States has been part of the problem not only by its unrelenting demand for drugs and its permissive arms market that has fueled arms trafficking and violence in Mexico, but also because of the pressure exerted on its southern neighbor to confront the cartels. According to US Bureau of Arms Tobacco and Firearms (ATF) data, 90–95% of guns used in drug violence in Mexico enter illegally from the United States; it is estimated that the several hundred arms entering Mexico per day add to the estimated 40 million illicit guns already in the country (Brands 2009: 20). The persistence of arms trafficking into Mexico is explained not only by the lack of political support in the United States for extending the Federal Assault Weapons Ban (AWB) in 2004 after ten years of observation (Koper, Woods, Roth and Shirk 2004), but also by the fact that 10% of US gun dealers are located on the Mexican border (Shirk 2011: 13). Currently, 70% of guns seized by Mexican authorities, submitted for tracing, have a US origin (Martinez 2019). However, the United States has not only contributed to violence in Mexico, but it has also been affected because of its own vulnerability to criminal activity of Mexican organizations operating both within its own territory through local gangs and south of the border (Maciel 2017).

In 2008, the United States and Mexico entered into an agreement called the "Merida Initiative" that was a three-year $1.4 billion US aid package to provide equipment and training, on top of an estimated $4 billion annually devoted by Mexico to the fight against drugs (Astorga and Shirk 2010: 25). This agreement was explained not only because of the strategic importance of Mexico in terms of the 2,000-mile common border and the variety of issues that are part of the complex bilateral relationship, such as US foreign direct investment, NAFTA, Mexico being a potential source of asylum seekers (Shirk 2011: 4–5), but also because of concerns emanating from south of the border such as organized crime, drug trafficking, terrorism, and insurgency (Gereben Schaefer, Bahney and Riley 2009: xv). It is important to note that US counter-narcotics aid to Mexico had previously amounted to around $55–60 million annually in the seven years since 2000 (Brands 2009: xv). In this context, if significant in comparison to previous periods, the Merida Initiative was relevant mainly because of its symbolism, in particular because of the US government's acceptance of the principle of "shared-responsibility" in reference to Mexico's drug-related violence, which represented a departure from the previous "finger-pointing" practice on the part of each other in the bilateral relationship. As a matter of fact, in one of her official visits to Mexico City, then-US Secretary of State, Hilary Clinton, conceded that the United States was in part responsible for violence in Mexico (Ellingwood 2009), and her statement had no precedent in the US discourse toward its neighbor to the south.

Nevertheless, militarization of anti-narcotics operations has continued to lead to an increase in human rights violations, as mentioned earlier, and it has contributed to corruption, to desertion within the rank and file of the Mexican military, and to more violence, in general (Astorga and Shirk 2010: 3). The most ominous sign of President Calderon's strategy, however, was the 50,000 deaths (Molzahn, Rios and

Shirk 2012) produced by the three-pronged confrontation (i.e. intra-DTO, DTO vs. DTO, and DTOs vs. government) that were directly attributed to the federal government's policy, even though the President repeatedly argued that far from initiating violence, the government only responded to what already was a violent situation (*Europa Press* 2012), a point which seems to have merit.

For instance, from the total death toll since 2006, 90% of homicides were estimated to be part of intra-criminal conflicts, without the authority being involved in any manner (Villalobos 2012: 7). It is important to note that even though violence has involved innocent civilians, such as in the case of grenades being thrown at a crowd in Morelia on Independence Day in 2008 (García 2008), criminal activity has not preeminently targeted civilians (Williams 2009: 2). Homicides are occurring precisely where there are disputes for *plazas* and corridors among criminal organizations, and those conflicts started before the presence of authorities was required (Villalobos 2012: 9). In this context, what produces and explains violence has not been the intervention of the federal government *per se*, but the intrinsic dynamic of crime as expressed in a high level of "criminal density" (Villalobos 2012: 1 and 7). Violence is evidence of growing criminal activities because of the government's long-time practice of managing, rather than solving, the problem in order to avoid conflict (Villalobos 2012: 1), and it is only in this sense that violence is an outcome created by a failed official strategy.

The situation has been so dire in Mexico, that at some point both official and private estimates pointed to the country's supposedly "failed state" status (Friedman 2008) and possibility for a "rapid and sudden collapse" (DoD 2008: 36). A more nuanced and accurate characterization of Mexico's predicament, nevertheless, made reference not to a "state failure", but to a "security failure", meaning that the Mexican government has been ineffective only in the security sphere but not as a state as a whole, which is different (Kenny, Serrano and Sotomayor 2012: 2–3). Even though the situation in Mexico has been far from stable, the country does not have the worst record of violence in the Western Hemisphere. For instance, between 2010 and 2017, the figure for homicides per 100,000 population went from 15.8 to 17.2 for the Americas; 22 to 30.5 for Brazil; 6.1 to 24.9 for Colombia; 76.1 to 41.7 for Honduras; and 22 to 24.8 for Mexico (UNODC 2019).

Most analysts agree that the US war on drugs is a failure that requires a new approach (see Global Commission on Drug Policy 2011), evident in the fact that drugs are more accessible, more widely utilized, and more potent than ever before (Astorga and Shirk 2010: 4).

Given that the US demand for drugs will continue and no possible modification of the US Constitution Second Amendment is in sight regarding the easy access to weapons in the United States, the option for the Mexican government is to continue fighting drug trafficking, perhaps through a more focused strategy targeting not HVTs, but the mid-level members of DTOs in order to erode their operational capacity (Felbab-Brown 2011: 44). It can be argued that the state cannot afford to have the state institutions challenged, and this is the reason why the offensive continued after Calderon, and also why advancing on the institution-building process is fundamental.

5.2 Increasing Exposure to the International Environment

Mexico is inserted, both by circumstances and choice, in the complex foreign environment of the 21st Century, and the country is exposed therefore to the political, military, economic, social, and environmental challenges that currently characterize world affairs.

Because of the size of its territory, population, economy, and natural resources, Mexico is one of the important actors in the international system, even though the country faces serious internal challenges. The country, for instance, has the 11th largest economy in the world and it is the 15th largest exporter (World Bank 2020). Mexico is required, therefore, to formulate a national security policy not only to diminish the vulnerabilities of its increasing external exposure, but also to take advantage of the international context to address its internal challenges. It requires a comprehensive strategy to confront these issues beyond its traditional concern about maintaining its autonomy vis-à-vis the United States, and the need to contain the domestic effects of drug-related violence.

Mexico's birth as an independent nation demanded a reaffirmation of its sovereignty, and from the beginning its foreign policy objectives consisted in upholding its autonomy and identity regarding hegemonic powers. At the end of the 19th and beginning of the 20th centuries, economic development also became a preeminent objective, and both were incorporated in the current 1917 Constitution as basic national interests, thus becoming the basis of its national security outlook and guidelines of its foreign policy as its preeminent national security instrument.

Mexico's history is the history of its relationship with the United States, and therefore the impact its neighbor to the north has had on Mexico's foreign policy is evident. In particular, the determinant role of the United States explains the country's foreign policy predominantly defensive posture, based on the principles of International Law. The promotion of these principles has been the result of Mexico's historical experience as the best defense for a weak nation, and they have also been reinforced by the Mexican active participation in multilateral forums, in particular the United Nations.

As a country with a single-party throughout the post-revolutionary period and no extensive links with the outside world, in the 1950s and 1960s, Mexico made the most out of its relative isolation as a result of post-WWII adjustments to promote industrialization. The external environment was not a priority for Mexican governments, other than the interest in the defense of the foreign policy principles and the promotion of multilateral goodwill. The exhaustion of the ISIS model in the 1960s, intensification of interdependence in the 1970s, and dramatic changes in international politics brought about by the fall of the Berlin wall and the collapse of the Soviet Union at the end of the 1980s and beginning of the 1990s represented not only the triumph of the liberal ideology, but also the intensification of the globalization process, forcing Mexican foreign policy to transform itself. This change was about promoting a more active role for the country in an increasingly globalized world, as well as seeking trade integration with the United States as the answer to the formation of regional trade blocs.

Efforts to expand Mexico's role abroad were intensified in the Salinas Administration by basically redefining the relationship with the United States through NAFTA, since diversifying the country's economic relations with other areas of the world was rather limited. Mexico, however, developed closer relations with key countries and in different multilateral forums. It went from being an economically closed country to one with the largest network of trade agreements, in the process expanding its exposure abroad.

This opening took place, nevertheless, without actually incorporating a national security perspective other than finding markets for Mexican products and gaining access to foreign investment. According to official information, Mexico currently has a network of 13 Free Trade Agreements (FTAs) with 50 countries, 32 Agreements for the Promotion and Reciprocal Protection of Investments (APRPIs) with 33 countries, and 9 "Partial Scope Agreements" within the framework of the Latin American Integration Association (ALADI). Furthermore, Mexico actively participates in multilateral and regional organizations and forums such as the World Trade Organization (WTO), the Asia-Pacific Economic Cooperation Mechanism (APEC), and the

Organization for Economic Cooperation and Development (OECD) (Gobierno de Mexico 2015).

In the Fox period, and with the idea of taking advantage of the "democratic bonus", the country adopted a foreign policy aimed at defending human rights, democracy, the environment and fighting corruption, and promoting a greater participation in multilateral forums and in defense of Mexican migrants in the United States. In this way, the country expanded its focus on international economic issues to include political affairs, even though it has been difficult to provide coherence between domestic and foreign policies to the extent that while human rights are defended abroad, they are violated in the country. Calderon focused on security matters, in particular on strengthening cooperation with the United States, as reflected in the Merida Initiative.

Peña-Nieto emphasized the economy as evident in the relevance assigned to his structural reforms. As established in his PND, its fifth goal was "Mexico with global responsibility" based on the idea that the country was an "emerging power". In this context, under Peña-Nieto, there was an intense diplomatic activity and investment in a communications campaign to improve the image of Mexico abroad, which had been eroded by former governments diplomatic decisions and insecurity and crime in the country (Ramirez Meda and Rochin Aguilar 2017: 54). This campaign to attract foreign investment, nevertheless, faced persistent corruption and insecurity, and serious cases of human rights violations in the country, such as Ayotzinapa and Tlatlaya, Guerrero, in 2014; Tanhuato, Michoacan, in 2015; and Nochixtlan, Oaxaca, in 2016.

Official documents identify several challenges for which the country has to be prepared for the future, reflecting its unequivocal exposure and vulnerability to developments abroad. For instance, protecting its biodiversity, and climate change and its impact on food and water security in the country are considered to be related, and in this context, Mexico adopted in 2013 a Climate Change National Strategy and a General Climate Change Law to reduce greenhouse emissions by 2020 (Mexico 2014: 86–8). The document, nevertheless, misses any specific foreign policy actions to mitigate the effects of this phenomenon in the future and even though there are actions taken, this important issue does not seem to be part of an integral strategic perspective.

In reference to energy security, even though it is recognized that both the United States and Canada are leading the energetic transformation of North America through becoming leaders in conventional and non-conventional hydrocarbon production, it establishes that if it is true that Mexico processes more oil than its demand, its production of secondary products is less than national consumption, and therefore the country could become a net importer of greater amounts of gas, gasoline, and diesel. This situation makes Mexico highly vulnerable to international oil prices such as currently when the price of oil dropped in the context of COVID-19, and therefore it is important to have a long-term perspective in this regard.

As a nation open to the world, commercial and tourism exchanges make Mexico more exposed to risks associated with the flow of people and goods, and therefore health is clearly an issue of national security, as well as the country being susceptible to national disasters and the need to promote resilience and mitigation of its effects. The document recognizes the link of national security to technology and innovation, and this is a step in the correct direction (Mexico 2014: 88–91).

Mexico currently faces important international transformations, a more aggressive US foreign policy, and more nationalist and conservative policies in the international context such as Brexit, for which the country needs to be prepared in order to promote its interests in a less collaborative international context. Nevertheless, at a time when there is in Mexico a president who considers that "the best foreign policy is domestic policy" (Hernandez 2018), at the same time the country requires its national interests to be actively defended abroad. For instance, regarding the caravan of migrants from Central America and the pressures of the Trump Administration to tighten security at the Mexican border, a second wave of US pressure to confront drug trafficking in the midst of a failure to contain violence in the country, and the security and economic challenge of the spread of COVID-19, cannot be ruled out. These issues clearly demand a comprehensive and long-term national security perspective to allow Mexico to respond to issues that originate abroad, and that increasingly have a greater impact domestically.

If it is true militarily that the country has not faced an immediate threat due to the aforementioned explanation, its geopolitical situation demands the country to professionalize its armed forces and to continue investing in its modernization and incorporation of new technologies. As part of the North American region and because of its implicit aligning to the United States, Mexico has to be prepared to face the consequences of scenarios where attempts to infringe on US national security by its adversaries can have a potential impact on Mexico's own national security.

5.3 Elements of a New Outlook

Even though Mexico has historically had a vulnerable international position due to its geographical location – by being the neighbor of a major power since the 19th Century – its security concerns have focused mainly on domestic challenges, which eventually led to its national security notion being dominated by internal issues.

If it is understandable that each country has its own national security outlook in accordance with its specific goals and challenges, in the case of Mexico, national security is dominated by domestic security concerns, but this orientation does not reflect the nature of the term. This situation represents a distortion in terms of the justification to directly involve its armed forces in public security activities, even though they were not created and trained to do so. This has only delayed the development of truly professional police forces to protect people and their property. The problem in Mexico regarding the armed forces participation in public security tasks is that the military has been exposed to the aforementioned corruption and human rights violations. This is a serious concern, since the armed forces guarantee the permanence of the state, and they also represent an institution that over the years has contributed to the stability of the country by maintaining its loyalty to the civilian leadership. This is the fundamental reason for protecting them and avoiding their exposure to tasks that, in principle, do not correspond to their professional formation.

Additional evidence of the distortion referred to earlier is not only the multiplicity of mentions made to Mexico's national security in public debates without knowledge about the subject, but the fact that this confusion is reflected in fundamental documents such as the LSN that is actually a legislation to regulate the civil intelligence agency of the Mexican state. In this regard, the distortion consists in equating national security to intelligence without distinguishing the difference between each one's scope, or the relationship between them, failing to understand that intelligence is one of the basic instruments to promote national security. Mexico, then, requires a true National Security Law to consolidate a national security system and strategy, where objectives are defined, as well as the possible obstacles to achieving those objectives and the means to overcome those obstacles. In this context, a separate law should be formulated for regulating intelligence activities.

One of the aspects that require reformulation to address current and future challenges is actually intelligence, and in this sense, it is important to transcend the idea that intelligence equals political espionage.

As vital information for the national security decision-making process, Mexico requires an external intelligence service under the Presidency to provide the Executive with timely and reliable information on the impact of international events. It is then necessary to create a separate foreign intelligence agency and to maintain the current intelligence institution, which predominately carries out domestic intelligence in the SSPC to address internal security challenges and to carry out counterintelligence duties to identify and neutralize the activities of foreign intelligence services operating in Mexican territory. Having separate external and internal intelligence agencies then entails the need for a National Intelligence System to coordinate each of the federal departments' units whose individual analyses require to be integrated in order to generate national estimates about a given issue.

While a Mexican foreign intelligence agency is built, it is essential, for instance, that SRE creates an intelligence unit that allows for the integration of all information produced daily by Mexico's representations abroad in order to have a global perspective on political, economic, social, and military issues around the world, and then incorporate this unit to the system referred to earlier once it is created. Even though SRE produces information like other foreign affairs ministries around the world, in the case of Mexico, this wealth of data is not used for the benefit of the decision-making process, nor viewed from a national security perspective. The creation of a foreign intelligence service then begs the question why Mexico needs such an institution, given its limited capacity to shape world developments. The answer is that, first of all, Mexico would not need to devote considerable resources to foreign intelligence because, in the context of the chaotic globalized 21st Century, what is required is the ability to "examining interconnections and feedback loops that can cause small developments to mutate into big dangers"; to tackle this kind of "emerging complex systems threats",

> Intelligence must operate on a smaller and smarter scale. It must rely less on secret information, and more on interdisciplinary teams of experts tasked with understanding the larger context of events… They must view their role as helping policymakers to identify variables they can influence, directly and indirectly, and to anticipate the possible impacts on the system of various policy options.
>
> (Rivkin and Beebe 2020)

Even if Mexico has only a limited ability to influence events abroad, it is extremely difficult to argue that the country would be better off without – than with – information.

An additional and necessary element, fundamental for the coordination of policies on this matter, is the operation of a National Security Council directly under the Presidency with a permanent staff of specialists on topics and areas of the world who provide information to the President on the most relevant issues abroad, and, in turn, advise the Executive and the members of the CSN regarding information that must be required of the intelligence agencies of the Mexican state. This is in line with the objective of creating a "Culture of Intelligence" to make the public aware of the vital role played by this kind of institutions (as opposed to political espionage), and thus creating the opportunity to attract talent, the best cadres of young professionals who wish to join the intelligence service.

Beyond voices that point out that Mexico is a country of peace that does not require armed forces (Medellin 2019), on the contrary, it is necessary to modernize and professionalize them because no country can face a potentially adverse international context without coercive instruments, if needed, and because the evolution of threats requires the guarantee provided by military power in the face of "an unpredictable period of strategic transition" (Kuper 2019). As already mentioned, Mexico is exposed to non-conventional, but also to conventional threats by being neighbor to the United States as the country's infrastructure or territory is susceptible to actions to affect US interests (Reyez and Camacho 2018). In this context, for instance, SEMAR should be taken out of anti-narcotics operations to strengthen instead the defense of the strategically important zone of the Gulf of Mexico and the Caribbean (Stratfor 2009), not to compete with the United States, but to complement US assets in the area. Historically, due to Mexico's difficult terrain, it has been complicated to mobilize forces within its territory, and therefore the development of local law enforcement forces, in this case municipal ones, is crucial to provide security (GPF Team 2018). Moreover, the Mexican government should offer the guarantee to the United States that it can take care of its own security in order not to be excluded from decisions susceptible to be taken anyway that affect the country (Tello Peon 2016: 395).

This strengthening of the armed forces involves separating them from public security tasks to maintain their capabilities, even though they are required to collaborate with domestic security tasks. They would do so by providing intelligence information via the National

Intelligence System and by providing platforms and infrastructure to law enforcement without dealing with domestic challenges directly, in order not to become contaminated. It also involves leaving behind the idea, more discursive than real (Interviews 2020), that the armed forces must be separated from civilians so as not to politicize the former, and actually strengthen collaboration between civilians and the military, each field contributing with its own abilities, in order to defend and promote national interests more efficiently. Attenuating this separation is part of promoting a Culture of National Security where an increasingly complex domestic and international context demands the state to have access to the best capabilities it can muster, both civilian and military, to comprehensively formulate a national security policy.

There must be a civil sector working along the military sector that is seen not as competitive, but complementary, as in advanced countries of the world. Even though the Army has the second highest level of public acceptance in the country (only below universities), with seven persons out of ten, the trust civilians have in the military sometimes unwittingly "puts an artificial distance between them", thus creating the myth – among the military – that military service is superior to any civilian background, eclipsing respect for other institutions and forms of service (Karlin and Hunt Friend 2018). This is not positive for democracy, nor for the complementarity referred to earlier.

Also related to armed forces matters, to the extent that the operational environment is becoming increasingly complex, Mexico requires to count on a Joint Chiefs of Staff that represents a reorganization of the military sector in the country. Instead of a separate Secretary of National Defense and Air Force and a Secretary of the Navy, there must be a single Secretary of Defense with three different departments to achieve a greater coordination and interoperability of systems, in order to improve the possibility of carrying out both joint and combined military operations.

Although a politically sensitive issue, this reorganization does not necessarily require Mexico to have a civilian Secretary of Defense. It just takes an agreement within the armed forces for rotation to take place among the leadership of the departments to assume this position. Countries in Latin America that now have civilian Secretaries of Defense have seen this transformation as part of transition of democracy in countries where the military have had a prominent political role, which is not the case of Mexico where its military has proven time and again to be highly institutional and loyal to the civilian elected officials.

The creation of this system is important because very contrary to the fact that in the future the country could isolate from the external context, it is most likely that the opposite will occur; that is, its exposure will increase.

Analyzing the timeline since the topic of national security began to be discussed in Mexico in the 1980s, until today, it is clear that there has been a limited but positive evolution. It is also evident that the bases for consolidating a system already exist, but what is missing to operate this system is the political will based on an undistorted understanding of what national security represents and of Mexico's position in the world.

An argument can be made about the incompatibility of refocusing national security in Mexico by going back to the basics (to the origin of the term being dominated by the state and military factors), because state threats are not the country's main security concerns. However, for the purpose of this analysis, "refocusing" national security in Mexico does not require making an apology of national security; on the contrary, de-securitizing issues is a far superior and effective course of action than securitizing (Buzan, Waever, and Wilde 1998: 29) and thus avoiding switching to an "extraordinary measures" mode. Moreover, as long as states remain the central elements of the international system, understanding national security is a fundamental task. According to a perspective,

> National security activities are now addressing a far wider array of phenomena than in the past, both in the Western world and beyond. We take as our starting point the assumption that national security cannot be completely divorced from "traditional" interpretations, in which policy is shaped by agencies, ministries and other institutions tasked with the protection of national interests from exogenous threats.
>
> (Sussex, Clarke and Medcalf 2017: 476)

By delimiting the concept and emphasizing its external character, therefore, this discussion's objective has been to put national security back in the box in order to bring order to a needed reorganization of national security in Mexico.

Bibliography

Astorga, L., and Shirk, D. A. (2010). *Drug Trafficking Organizations and Counter-Drug Strategies in the U.S.-Mexican Context.* Mexico and the

United States: Confronting the Twenty-First Century. USMEX WP 10-0. Center for U.S.-Mexican Studies, School of International Relations and Pacific Studies, University of California, San Diego (USMEX), El Colegio de la Frontera Norte (Tijuana), Woodrow Wilson International Center for Scholars, El Colegio de México. Retrieved from: http://usmex.ucsd.edu/assets/024/11632.pdf

Beittel, J. S. (January 7, 2011). *Mexico's Drug Trafficking Organizations: Source and Scope of Rising Violence.* Prepared for Members and Committees of Congress, Congressional Research Service (CRS). Retrieved from: http://fpc.state.gov/documents/organization/155587.pdf

Brands, H. (May, 2009). *Mexico's Narco-Insurgency and US Counterdrug Policy.* Strategic Studies Institute. United States Army War College (USAWAC). Retrieved from: http://www.strategicstudiesinstitute.army.mil/pubs/summary.cfm?q=918

Buzan, B., Waever, O., and de Wilde, J. (1998). *Security: A New Framework for Analysis.* Boulder, CO: Lynne Rienner Publishers.

Calderon-Hinojosa, F. (2010). *La Lucha por la Seguridad Pública.* Presidencia de la Republica. Retrieved from: http://portal.sre.gob.mx/chicago/pdf/061810SeguridadPublica.pdf

Cerda-Ardura, A. (October 11, 2011). "Los Matazetas, Apuesta por Mayor Violencia". Entrevista a Luis Astorga Almanza/Investigador del Instituto de Investigaciones Sociales de la UNAM. *Siempre!* Retrieved from: http://www.siempre.mx/2011/10/los-matazetas-apuesta-por-mayor-violencia/

Ellingwood, K. (March 26, 2009). "US Shares Blame for Mexico Drug Violence, Clinton Says". *Los Angeles Times.* Retrieved from: http://www.latimes.com/news/nationworld/world/la-fg-mexico-clinton26-2009mar26,0,2128382.story

Europa Press. (February 16, 2012). "Calderon Justifica el Despliegue de Militares en Rregiones con Violencia 'Inmanejable'". Retrieved from: http://www.europapress.es/latam/mexico/noticia-mexico-calderon-justificadespliegue-militares-regiones-donde-violencia-inmanejable-20120216215447.html

Felbab-Brown, V. (September, 2011). *Calderon's Caldron. Lessons from Mexico's Battle against Organized Crime and Drug Trafficking in Tijuana, Ciudad Juarez, and Michoacán.* Latin America Initiative. Brookings Institution. Retrieved from: https://www.brookings.edu/wp-content/uploads/2016/06/09_calderon_felbab_brown.pdf

Felbab-Brown, V. (March, 2009). *The Violent Drug Market in Mexico and Lessons from Colombia.* Policy Paper Number 12. Foreign Policy at Brookings, The Brookings Institution. Retrieved from: https://www.brookings.edu/wp-content/uploads/2016/06/03_mexico_drug_market_felbabbrown.pdf

Friedman, G. (May 13, 2008). "Mexico: On the Road to Failed State?" *Stratfor.* Free Podcast. Retrieved from: http://www.stratfor.com/weekly/mexico_road_failed_state

Garcia, A. K. (December 16, 2019). "La Economia Informal Genero 22 de Cada 100 Pesos del PIB de Mexico en 2018". *El Economista.* Retrieved from:

https://www.eleconomista.com.mx/economia/La-economia-informal-genero-22-de-cada-100-pesos-del-PIB-de-Mexico-en-2018-20191216-0033.html

García, M. (September 16, 2008). "Grenade Attacks Kill 8 on Mexico's National Day". *Reuters*. Retrieved from: http://www.reuters.com/article/2008/09/16/us-mexico-blasts-idUSN1634595120080916

Gereben Schaefer, A., Bahney, B., and Riley, K. J. (2009). *Security in Mexico. Implications for US Policy Options*. RAND, Monograph Series. Santa Monica, CA: RAND Corporation. Retrieved from: http://www.insyde.org.mx/images/security_in_mexico.pdf

Global Commission on Drug Policy. (June, 2011). *War on Drugs. Report of the Global Commission on Drug Policy*. Retrieved from: http://www.globalcommissionondrugs.org/wpcontent/themes/gcdp_v1/pdf/Global_Commission_Report_English.pdf

Gobierno de Mexico. (May 10, 2015). *Comercio Exterior/Países con Tratados y Acuerdos Firmados por Mexico*. Secretaria de Economia. Retrieved from: https://www.gob.mx/se/acciones-y-programas/comercio-exterior-paises-con-tratados-y-acuerdos-firmados-con-mexico

GPF Team. (March 15, 2018). "Mexico: A History of Power Vacuums". *Geopolitical Futures*. Retrieved from: https://geopoliticalfutures.com/mexico-history-power-vacuums/

Grayson, G. W. (2015). *The Los Zetas Drug Cartel. Sadism as an Instrument of Cartel Warfare in Mexico and Central America*. San Diego, CA: Published by Didactic Press.

Hernandez, G. (May 20, 2018). "La Mejor Política Exterior es la Interior: AMLO". *SDPnoticias.com*. Retrieved from: https://www.sdpnoticias.com/nacional/interior-exterior-politica-mejor-amlo.html

Infobae. (October 18, 2019). "Este es el Mapa del Narcotrafico en Mexico a 10 Meses de la Llegada de Lopez Obrador". Retrieved from: https://www.infobae.com/america/mexico/2019/10/19/este-es-el-mapa-del-narcotrafico-en-mexico-a-10-meses-de-la-llegada-de-lopez-obrador-al-poder/

Interviews carried out on February 25, 2020 in Mexico City with high-ranking officials from Centro de Estudios Superiores Navales (CESNAV) and Colegio de Defensa Nacional (CODENAL).

Karlin, M., and Hunt Friend, A. (September 24, 2018). "Military Worship Hurts US Democracy". *Brookings*. Retrieved from: https://www.brookings.edu/blog/order-from-chaos/2018/09/24/military-worship-hurts-us-democracy/

Kenny, P., and Serrano, M. (Eds.), with Sotomayor, A. (2012). *Mexico's Security Failure. Collapse into Criminal Violence*. New York, NY: Routledge.

Koper, C. S., with Woods, D. J., and Roth, J. A. (June 2004). An Updated Assessment of the Federal Assault Weapons Ban: Impacts on Gun Markets and Gun Violence, 1994–2003. Report to the National Institute of Justice with funds from the U.S. Department of Justice (DoJ). Document No. 204431. Jerry Lee Center of Criminology, University of Pennsylvania. Retrieved from: https://www.ncjrs.gov/pdffiles1/nij/grants/204431.pdf

Kuper, S. (2019). "Dibb Report 2.0: Paul Dibb enters the 'Defending Australia Debate'". *Defence Connect*. Retrieved from: https://www.defence

connect.com.au/key-enablers/4961-dibb-report-2-0-paul-dibb-enters-the-defending-australia-debate

Maciel, A. (May, 2017). "'Project Deliverance': A Case Study of the Relevance of Task Forces against Transnational Criminal Organizations in US-Mexican Relations". *Anuario Latinoamericano. Ciencias Políticas y Relaciones Internacionales*. Vol. 4. Retrieved from: file:///C:/Users/einformatica/Downloads/5428-3721.pdf

Martinez, G. (July 7, 2019). "The Flow of Guns from the US to Mexico Is Getting Lost in the Border Debate". *PBS/Newshour*. Retrieved from: https://www.pbs.org/newshour/politics/the-flow-of-guns-from-the-u-s-to-mexico-is-getting-lost-in-the-border-debate

Medellin, A. (July 4, 2019). "Lopez Obrador: 'Si Por Mi Fuera, Desapareceria al Ejercito y lo Convertiria en Guardia Nacional'". *Defensa.com*. Retrieved from: https://www.defensa.com/mexico/lopez-obrador-fuera-desapareceria-ejercito-convertiria-guardia

Mexico Evalua. (2018). *Hallazgos 2017. Seguimiento y Evaluacion del Sistema de Justicia Penal en Mexico*. Centro de Analisis de Politicas Publicas. Retrieved from: https://www.mexicoevalua.org/mexicoevalua/wp-content/uploads/2020/03/hallazgos2017.pdf

Mexico. Presidencia de la Republica. (2014). *Programa para la Seguridad Nacional 2014–2018. Una política multidimensional para México en el Siglo XXI*. Consejo de Seguridad Nacional. Retrieved from: https://www.resdal.org/caeef-resdal/assets/mexico----programa-para-la-seguridad-nacional.pdf

Molzahn, C, Rios, V., and Shirk, D. A. (March, 2012). *Drug Violence in Mexico. Data and Analysis through 2011*. Special Report, Trans-Border Institute, Joan B. Kroc School of Peace Studies, University of San Diego. Retrieved from: http://justiceinmexico.files.wordpress.com/2012/03/2012-tbi-drug violence.pdf

Monroy, M. (February 2, 2011). "Empleo Informal, un Lastre para Mexico". *CNNExpansion.com*. Retrieved from: http://www.cnnexpansion.com/mi-carrera/2011/02/02/empleo-informal-mexico-seguro-social-cnn

O'Neil, S. (Spring, 2010). "Mexico-U.S. Relations: What's Next?" *Americas Quarterly*.

Ramirez Meda, K., and Rochin Aguilar, N. M. (2017). "La Politica Exterior de Mexico durante el Sexenio de Peña Nieto". *Comillas Journal of International Relations*. No. 8. Retrieved from: https://revistas.comillas.edu/index.php/internationalrelations/article/view/7786/7595

Rawlins, A. (December 13, 2011). *Mexico's Drug War*, Council on Foreign Relations (CFR). Retrieved from: http://www.cfr.org/mexico/mexicos-drug-war/p13689

Reyez J., and Camacho, Z. (October 22, 2018), "Intervencion Militar Extranjera, la Mayor Vulnerabilidad de Mexico". *Contralinea*. Retrieved from: https://www.contralinea.com.mx/archivo-revista/2018/10/22/intervencion-militar-extranjera-la-mayor-vulnerabilidad-de-mexico/

Rivkin, D. B. Jr. and Beebe, G. S. (March 31, 2020). "Before This Pandemic Ends, Intel Agencies Should Prepare for a World of Threats". *The Hill.* Retrieved from: https://thehill.com/opinion/national-security/490160-before-this-pandemic-ends-intel-agencies-should-prepare-for-a-world-of-threats

Salmeron, I. (February 13, 2006). "A Muerte, la Lucha de los Capos por Dominar el Narcotrafico". Entrevista a Luis Astorga Almanza y Jorge Chabat/Investigadores sociales. *Siempre!*

Shirk, D. A. (March, 2011). *The Drug War in Mexico. Confronting a Shared Threat*, Center for Preventive Action, Council on Foreign Relations. Council Special Report No. 60. Retrieved from: www.cfr.org/content/publications/attachments/Mexico_CSR60.pdf

Stratfor. (November 17, 2009). *The Geopolitics of Mexico: A Mountain Fortress Besieged.* Assessments. Stratfor Monographs on the Geopolitics of Countries Influential in World Affairs. Retrieved from: https://worldview.stratfor.com/article/geopolitics-mexico-mountain-fortress-besieged

Sussex, M., Clarke, M., and Medcalf, R. (August 8, 2017). "National Security: Between Theory and Practice". *Australian Journal of International Affairs.* Vol. 71, No. 5. Retrieved from: https://www.tandfonline.com/doi/full/10.1080/10357718.2017.1347139

Tello Peon, J. E. (2016). "Seguridad Nacional y Politica Exterior: Espacios para la Acción". In L. Herrera-Lasso (Ed.), *Mexico ante el Mundo: Tiempo de Definiciones* (p. 395). Seccion de Obras de Politica y Derecho. Mexico: Fondo de Cultura Economica.

United Nations Office on Drugs and Crime (UNODC). (2019). *Global Study on Homicide 2019.* United Nations. Retrieved from: https://www.unodc.org/unodc/en/data-and-analysis/global-study-on-homicide.html

US Department of Defense (DoD). *The Joint Operational Environment 2008.* United States Joint Forces Command, Center for Joint Futures (J59). Retrieved from: http://www.jfcom.mil/newslink/storyarchive/2008/JOE2008.pdf

US Department of Justice (DoJ). (December, 2008). *National Drug Threat Assessment 2009*, National Drug Intelligence Center (NDIC). Retrieved from: http://www.justice.gov/ndic/pubs31/31379/31379p.pdf

US Department of Justice (DoJ). (August, 2011). *National Drug Threat Assessment 2011*, National Drug Intelligence Center (NDIC). Retrieved from: http://www.justice.gov/ndic/pubs44/44849/44849p.pdf

Villalobos, J. (January 1, 2010). "Doce Mitos de la Guerra Contra el Narco". *Nexos* en línea. Retrieved from: http://www.nexos.com.mx/?P=leerarticulo&Article=72941

Villalobos, J. (January 1, 2012). "Nuevos mitos de la guerra contra el narco". *Nexos.* Retrieved from: http://www.nexos.com.mx/?P=leerarticulo&Article=2102505

Williams, P. (April, 2009). "Drug Trafficking, Violence, and the State in Mexico". *Op-Ed*, Strategic Studies Institute, U.S. Army War College (USAWC). Retrieved from: http://www.strategicstudiesinstitute.army.mil/pdffiles/pub913.pdf

The World Bank. (April 13, 2020). "Mexico Overview". *The World Bank in Mexico.* Retrieved from: https://www.worldbank.org/en/country/mexico/overview

Zepeda-Lecuona, G. R. (November 27, 2019). "El Mapa de la Violencia Homicida en Mexico". *Milenio.* Retrieved from: https://www.milenio.com/opinion/guillermo-raul-zepeda-lecuona/laberinto-de-la-legalidad/el-mapa-de-la-violencia-homicida-en-mexico

Conclusions

The purpose of this analysis was to explore the reasons why Mexico lacks an integral, long-term, national security perspective, and the answer to this question was the existence of a confusion regarding the distinction among "national", "internal", and "public" security, which has led the country to maintain an inward-looking view, focusing in the last decades on the challenge posed by drug-related violence.

As a result of the imperative to deal with drug trafficking, the government has mixed the instruments to confront this challenge, as the armed forces have been the primary instrument to deal with organized crime, rather than relying on professional law enforcement institutions. In this process, the military has been exposed to corruption and human rights violations. It is suggested, therefore, that as long as this confusion remains unaddressed, the country will not be able to reform its security sector, in a context in which Mexico requires not only to confront a dire internal security situation, but also an increasing exposure to developments originating beyond its borders.

Reforming the security sector in Mexico requires to understand, first of all, national security as a key concept of political realism, a dominant IR school of thought that emphasizes the central role of the state and military power in the international politics. The origin of realism and national security as its by-product are inextricably linked to the external environment and, therefore, this underlines its inadequacy to describe internal security challenges. However, this is what actually occurs in Mexico as the concept of national security is often used in reference to issues that can be best described as either internal or public security matters.

National security is a relatively recent subject in Mexico whose discussion was delayed by both the discredit of the concept in South America during the Cold War, and the need to prevent the United States from identifying its security interests with those of its neighbor to the south. In this context, the country has a predominantly inward-looking "national security" perspective explained by both its geo-political situation and the demilitarization of its political system. Nevertheless, the opening of its economy since the mid-1980s and a closer economic relationship with the United States have increasingly exposed Mexico to external developments and, therefore, it requires to adapt its national security perspective accordingly.

Determined by a strong presidentialism and an authoritarian nature that did not recede with democratic change, national security in Mexico has traditionally been defined by the President, according to the defense of the sovereignty and economic development objectives established in the constitution, and reflected in the six-year-term development plans of each administration. Even though the 2005 LSN is the main official document articulating national security in Mexico, this piece of legislation is actually misleading, because far from establishing and regulating a system, it is rather oriented to provide a legal framework to limit the activities of the Mexican civilian intelligence agency. One of the sources of confusion in Mexico about national security, moreover, is the fact that misunderstanding is built into the legislation, as the concept of national security comprises internal security, in the process mixing up the instruments at the disposal of the state to address challenges, in particular, contemplating the use of the armed forces to deal with domestic problems.

The basis of the national security structure in the country has been, at least since 1988, either the National Security Cabinet or the National Security Council, which have been kept as purely deliberative bodies. In Mexico, the guidelines for a national security system had been already established since 2009 through the National Security Programs describing the roles of the different agencies participating in the national security decision-making process, and for this reason the challenge, therefore, is not the absence of a framework, but the lack of political will and long-term vision to make the system work.

Drug trafficking represents a complication for Mexico's security because of its transformation, from a health issue to a public security matter, and into a national security threat, in the process of mixing up the coercive instruments of the state to the point where the military, a national security instrument par excellence to deter foreign threats, has been deployed to the streets to deal with organized crime on the country's urban and rural areas, without effectively containing the challenge.

Drug-related violence has been the most pressing domestic security challenge in Mexico. A review of President Calderon's period showed that it became a turning point in the country in terms of the fragmentation of criminal groups and dispersion of illicit activities, which are the main characteristics of the current security context. Furthermore, Mexico's increasing external exposure as a result not only of its accession to NAFTA, but to the diversification of its trade networks and increasing multilateral political activism in the context of globalization, is evidence of the country's vulnerability to developments beyond its borders for which it has not even the possibility of exerting marginal influence under the current circumstances.

In order to face both its domestic and external security environments, the security reform in Mexico must be based on a correct understanding of the nature of the national security concept. Notwithstanding the need to incorporate a greater external orientation imposed by the reality of a country that is increasingly open and exposed to developments abroad, this evolution has not been reflected in the design of a balanced national security policy, even though on paper, official documents reflect a greater concern for the exterior. This situation leaves Mexico vulnerable to the possibility of foreign security visions being imposed on the country, unrelated to its national interests.

Times have long been past when the topic of national security was considered to be taboo in Mexican politics and academia. National security is not only related to the threats a country faces, but also to the opportunities it loses if there is no vision translated into politics. If not having this policy represents a risk, having it could also be a risk if it is not based on a clear definition, which demonstrates why it is important to move forward in the discussion and analysis of national security in Mexico.

Restructuring Mexico's security sector to better adapt it to the 21st-century challenges requires clarity regarding the concept of national security and recognizes its fundamental external dimension, not to confuse it with internal and public security. This distinction is crucial to identifying and developing the adequate instruments to confront the specific challenges the country faces.

Not understanding the nature of national security represents an obstacle to reform security institutions in Mexico, and to accord them the relevance they deserve. Separating national from internal security would allow the country to restructure its national security sector, such as creating a foreign intelligence service, a National Security Council with a permanent staff, and a Joint Chiefs of Staff under a unified Secretary of Defense, as crucial elements of a much-needed modernization process in the country. The COVID-19 pandemic is just a reminder of how crucial it is to pay attention to the external environment, and how important it is to align Mexico's capabilities to confront a new and more challenging external reality.

The idea of reforming national security has the purpose of de-securitizing issues, which is a far more superior course of action than securitizing challenges without a clear grasp of the concept.

Index

Note: **Bold** page numbers refer to tables.